Hispanic Stars Rising

VOLUME IV

THE NEW FACE OF POWER

Hispanic Stars Rising Vol. IV

For more information, contact:

We Are All Human | www.weareallhuman.org
Hispanic Star | www.hispanicstar.org
Fig Factor Media, LLC | www.figfactormedia.com

Layout by LDG Juan Manuel Serna Rosales
Printed in the United States of America

ISBN: 978-1-959989-73-8
Library of Congress Control Number: 2023918368

To my loving family, who have always been there for me and helped me to achieve my dreams.

To the women who have inspired me, who have paved the way for me, and who have shown me that anything is possible.

To my late mother, who taught me the importance of hard work, education, and family.

And to the young Latinas who are the future of our community. I hope this book inspires you to reach your full potential and make your mark on the world.

This year, I dedicate this book to my son Joshua, who is studying computer science at Rice University. He is a brilliant young man with a bright future ahead of him.

To my daughter Tamara, who will be finishing high school soon. She is an incredible volleyball player and a kind and compassionate young woman.

And to my partner in crime, my husband Richard, whose love and belief in me gives me joy and strength. He is my best friend and the love of my life.

I am so grateful for all of you. We are making history together. Let's keep shining.

Table of Contents

ACKNOWLEDGMENTS
CLAUDIA ROMO EDELMAN

Year four—and the stories keep coming. When we first published *Hispanic Stars Rising*, the idea was to narrate our collective journey by sharing the individual paths people carve out to build their lives. We are so pleased that more and more people want to be part of this series. to share their Latinidad, their history, and the road they traveled to become who they are.

I thank all of you for sharing your stories. You have written your histories with all the twists and turns you have taken to realize your dreams. It is joyous to see people embrace their Latinidad more openly, more confidently, and with greater success. It is particularly gratifying to see people overcome challenges sometimes with little else than sheer will and determination propelling them forward. Each story is a treasure.

Together, they write the larger story of our diverse Hispanic community.

Five years ago, the We Are All Human Foundation began our work. We got past the early growing pains, past the long shadow of COVID-19, and we feel real traction today.

We are changing hearts and minds, slowly but surely. One thing is certain. The We Are All Human Team brings passion and persistence to all that we do from creating this book—which is a huge undertaking—to making sure that we are opening doors, finding support in Corporate America, and helping people become their best selves and remain true to themselves. I am so grateful to the team.

Our community continues to face challenges but we are moving forward.

Certainly, the stories in this volume speak to our continued progress. We will not stop until we are all seen, heard, and valued.

FOREWORD

DOLORES HUERTA

At the vantage point of 93 years, I can look back on my own path and see a certain inevitability — how one thing led to another, how one experience proliferated many others. The most rewarding journeys never follow a straight path. But ultimately, they made sense. You can see the purpose carried throughout.

My father, Juan Fernandez, was a farmworker, miner, salesman, veteran (World War 2 and the Korean War) and a representative in the New Mexico legislature. My parents divorced and my mother, Alicia St. John Chavez, worked two jobs to be able to start her own business, first a restaurant then a seventy-room hotel. She provided my siblings and I a middle class upbringing and education.

I was fortunate to learn about grassroots organizing from Fred Ross, Sr. who organized Latinos to desegregate schools in Westminster, California.[1,2] As a school teacher, seeing students malnourished and poor, I decided to leave teaching. I felt it would help farm worker families better to organize them to overcome their oppressive conditions. The farm worker's working conditions were terrible; low wage, no bathrooms, no drinking water. The farm workers were people of color, mostly Latinos.

The country, while being fed by the labors of these essential workers, is often oblivious to the injustices they faced. Successes were life changing. Understanding the discrimination against

---

[1] Sandra Robbie. *Mendez vs Westminster: For All the Children (Documentary Released 2003)*.
[2] Gabriel Thompson. *America's Social Arsonist: Fred Ross and Grassroots Organizing in the Twentieth Century* (University of California Press, 2016).

farmworkers began to open my eyes about other human rights more broadly—from the civil rights movement to the rise of feminism, then later, to LGBTQ+ rights. There was always — and continues to be — much work in ending injustice. And beyond that in making life better for the next generation.

When I look at the Latino community today, I feel tremendous pride. More and more we know that we are a community. And we act as a community, embracing our own diversity, unified by our hard work, perseverance, belief in education and the everlasting love of family and community. These values drive us forward.

More and more we are emboldened by our achievements. Importantly, taking credit for them. That is how, more and more, we get acknowledged for our contributions. Purpose gives us pride. Pride is essential to progress. And progress gives us a taste of even greater possibility. Reading through the stories of Latinos in this worthy volume, I am proud of the tenacity, inventiveness and courage of the people who share their stories. So many different lives, varying histories, and interesting paths. So much success against the odds. When we believe in ourselves, obstacles can be overcome. When we believe in others and join with them, we are unstoppable. That, I think, is one of the great takeaways from *Hispanic Stars Rising.*

The need to see not only the individual paths, but the collective journey. And most notably and honorably, it shows us how necessary it is to pay it forward. How important it is to see ourselves in a larger context, helping to right wrongs, level the playing field, and work towards what still needs to be fought; stronger — together.

Most of all *Hispanic Stars Rising* is a treasure trove of hope. Read it, learn from it, be proud of what has been achieved. But also keep going. Engage with the world. Your example of success will uplift others.

Feel your power as a community. Keep driving change.

Purpose is fueled by consistency, hard work and the willingness to take risks. ¡Sí se puede!

SPECIAL FOREWORD
DIANA FLORES

As I sit down to write these words, I am reminded of the journey that brought me here, to this very moment, where I find myself as the foreword author of this book, "Hispanic Stars Rising." It is a journey that has been both unexpected and profoundly fulfilling, one that has carried me from the flag football fields of Mexico City to the grand stages of the world. But more importantly, it is a journey that has allowed me to discover the power of dreams, of determination, and of the incredible strength within the Hispanic community.

You see, this was never my dream. As a young girl growing up in Mexico City, I embarked on a path that defied societal norms. At the tender age of eight, I began playing flag football—a sport largely considered to be the domain of men. It was in those early days that I first encountered the word "no" in its many forms. No, you can't play this sport. No, you will never amount to anything. No, no, no.

I yearned for a role model who looked like me, someone who had walked a similar path and broken through the barriers that seemed unbeatable. But there were none to be found, not because there weren't incredible Hispanic women excelling in sports, but because we were hidden in the shadows, our voices silenced.

It wasn't until last year when my team and I stood atop the podium, honored with gold medals from the World Games 2022, that I truly grasped the significance of our accomplishment. Those medals were not just symbols of our hard work and dedication;

they were seeds of inspiration down in the hearts of young girls and women. Much like this book, they were a testament to the fact that dreams, no matter how audacious, can become a reality.

The Hispanic community is a community of gold. We are filled with boundless potential, that like a precious metal, it takes time and effort to reveal it. I hope this book serves as a catalyst for that discovery.

Later on, when I had the privilege of being part of a Super Bowl commercial, I witnessed the power of storytelling firsthand. The message of women's empowerment, unity, and the breaking of stereotypes resonated with people from all walks of life. For many, it was the first time they heard their language spoken on such a grand stage. It underscored the importance of culture, family, and dreams, themes that are woven into the fabric of this book.

I feel truly blessed to have become a source of inspiration for future generations, especially considering that I was once that little girl searching for someone who looked like me in the spotlight. However, I am aware that my story is just one among many. Within the pages of this book, you will find a world of narratives—stories of resilience, triumph, and unyielding spirit.

If you are not a part of the Hispanic community, I invite you to open these pages and acquaint yourself with the richness of our heritage. It is crucial to recognize that the time has come not only to discuss inclusion but to take meaningful action in order to ensure that our community feels embraced, valued, and heard. Such efforts will undoubtedly pave the way for a brighter and more inclusive future for everyone.

If you are part of the Hispanic community, remember that now is the time to recognize that we are capable of dreaming bigger than ever before. You cannot dream about something you cannot see. Within the stories contained here, I hope you find the vision, the inspiration, and the motivation to dream your own dreams, and in doing so, become a star in your own right. Together, let us rise, shine, and transform perceptions. This is our time.

INTRODUCTION
CLAUDIA ROMO EDELMAN

This marks the fourth year that we are publishing *Hispanic Stars Rising*. Each volume has shared the individual stories of Hispanics—with different backgrounds, a deep and broad range of ambitions, and against all kinds of challenges—as they pursue and realize their dreams. Together, we transmit the collective experience of our Hispanic community, our own story told by ourselves.

It is quite a different and positive tale than the bleaker and negative one that has been not only merchandised too often but accepted as the truth. While the data about Hispanics tells a great story of prosperity, power, and progress, the common perceptions are still too often grounded in fears and untruths about immigrants, crime, and poverty.

Bad stories are amplified well beyond their actual import and impact. Good stories don't make great headlines. It is truly up to us to flip the script. The more we tell our stories, the more we control our own narrative, the greater control we will have over our future.

First, we have to understand our own power. Our gross domestic product (GDP) is $2.8 trillion, right behind Germany and ahead of the United Kingdom, India, France, Italy and Canada. We would be the 5th largest economy in the world and among the fastest growing. Our purchasing power is in excess of $2 trillion. We are the fastest-growing and second-largest segment in the country, and represent 26 percent of the total youth population, a huge indicator of our future strength. We lead the nation in upward mobility, with income growth at 77 percent and home ownership growth of 28 percent. We start more businesses than any other group in the nation—86 percent of all new businesses—and have held that position for the past ten years. One out of five entrepreneurs are Latino. We lead in technology startups. Our businesses hire 3 million workers to the tune of a $100 billion annual payroll. We are getting more bachelor and graduate degrees than ever before and, in turn, higher paying jobs.

Yet we are still struggling to leverage our own power. We are still not seen, heard, and valued. Representation may be increasing, but not as quickly or broadly as it should. In short, as a community, we still are not getting back anywhere near what we give. One of the reasons is that it is important to feel our collective strength so that we can leverage it.

Five years ago, the We Are All Human Foundation did a major research project, the Hispanic Sentiment Study. It was a temperature check on how Hispanics view our status and state of mind. In the summer of 2023, we released a five-year update. The findings are interesting though somewhat disturbing.

Despite all the tangible progress, the 2023 Hispanic Sentiment Study shows our frustration. One of the most disturbing pieces of data was that Hispanics feel excluded from the American narrative. Five years ago, 68 percent of our community felt that our values are shared and reflected by a majority of Americans. That percentage has since dropped to 42 percent. At the same time, however, fewer Latinos feel that the community is undervalued; 53 percent felt that way before and that statistic has dropped to 43 percent.

At the same time, we are more unified and prouder than ever. In 2018, 48 percent of Latinos felt we were unified as a community. Since then, that has jumped 7 points to 55 percent. Latino pride has increased from 61 percent to 64 percent. And a statistic I find really interesting and significant is that we are reclaiming our Latinidad, not simply in terms of culture, family, food, and values, like hard work, but also in terms of Spanish. Despite the fact that at least 80 percent of our community are American citizens and so many of them are young, the Spanish language is on the rise. Five years ago, 63 percent of Latinos included Spanish as a defining characteristic of our community, this year it has jumped to 77 percent. The Spanish language is on the rise. We are 100 percent American, our contributions to American society continue to build. We also are proud to be 100 percent Hispanic, too. We do not see it as a conflict.

Yet, representation across all public and private sectors is still not keeping pace with our accomplishments. We must keep working as a united community. We must keep telling our stories, individually and collectively. We are flipping the script. And all of the people represented in this book play a role in our collective strength and progress. This is our story, our narrative, our progress. We are proud to see these Hispanic Stars shine.

Author Stories

BREAKING GROUND, SHATTERING CEILINGS

JESSICA ACOSTA

"I am not defined by my circumstances; I am a product of my determination."

In a world where challenges can either break us or make us stronger, my story stands as a testament to resilience and determination. Born in Mexico and raised in humble beginnings, I defied the odds and carved my own path to success in the male-dominated construction industry.

Growing up as the middle child of three girls, I was raised in a tight-knit family that instilled in me the values of hard work. At fourteen, I immigrated to Denver, Colorado, facing the daunting task of adapting to a new country and language. After enrolling at West High School—one of two English as a second language (ESL) schools—I embarked on a journey of self-discovery and growth.

Despite encountering cultural shock and discrimination,

my drive for success remained. I pursued higher education at the University of Denver, majoring in Mass Communications. Balancing academic achievements with financial responsibilities, I took a receptionist job in the construction industry, diving headfirst into a male-dominated field that would shape my extraordinary journey.

With unwavering determination, I navigated the construction industry.

In the aftermath of the 2008 economic downturn, I faced a layoff as a project manager. I embraced change and recognized the opportunity within the chaos. In 2011, I embarked on a new venture, starting my own company that specialized in environmental compliance consulting for general contractors. This marked the beginning of my journey as a serial entrepreneur.

Fueled by my vision and passion, my entrepreneurial spirit soared. In 2017, I turned a dream into reality and launched the first coworking space for women in construction in Colorado. Empowering women became my driving force.

Beyond my own ventures, I dedicated myself to giving back to the community. Serving as a mentor for scaling businesses and as a board member for various organizations, I embodied the essence of servant leadership. My dedication earned me numerous accolades, including the prestigious Denver Business Journal's 40 Under 40 and Outstanding Businesswoman titles.

Believing in the power of innovation, I identified a need within the construction industry and developed a groundbreaking digital construction-technology, or contech, solution for environmental compliance inspections. My ability to envision and bring innovative solutions to life solidified my reputation as a visionary and trailblazer.

But my journey isn't just about awards and accomplishments; it's about embodying resilience, resourcefulness, and servant leadership. With charisma and natural intelligence, I inspired others to embrace their dreams, overcome obstacles, and create their own paths to success.

As a first-generation Latina immigrant, I transformed myself into a self-made entrepreneur, leaving an indelible mark on the construction and technology industries. I live by this quote: "The power to transform your life lies within you. I am not defined by my circumstances; I am a product of my determination."

In a world that often limits opportunities based on gender or background, my story serves as a reminder that breaking ground is possible. I encourage others to believe in their abilities and embrace their uniqueness. Together, we can redefine the norms and create a more inclusive future.

BIOGRAPHY

Jessica Acosta is the founder and CEO of Environmental Consulting Services (ECS), Acosta Group, and EDIFICE2120. As a serial entrepreneur and accomplished leader with significant experience in guiding diverse business operations, she has over twenty years of progressive experience in the construction industry and exceptional judgment to execute intricate projects. Jessica's track record shows that she is a recognized business leader within the construction industry, as well as across other industries and in the community. She is exceedingly community-minded; deeply ingrained in her DNA is her desire to give back, therefore she has served on several community boards and boards of advisors. Currently, Jessica sits on several committees for the Hispanic Contractors of Colorado and serves as a board member on the Denver Metro Chamber Leadership Foundation. Her outstanding record of service to the community and her remarkable business acumen have been recognized as one of Colorado's younger leading entrepreneurs by the Denver Business Journal with the 2014 Forty under Forty award and by the ColoradoBiz Magazine as one of the Top 5 Most Influential Professionals. Moreover, the Denver Business Journal accredited Jessica as one of Denver's most influential business leaders with the Outstanding Women in Business award. She holds a Bachelor of Science degree in communications and a minor in psychology from the University of Denver. She holds a diploma as a Safety and Health Specialist of Stormwater from Red Rocks Community College among other stormwater certifications. Additionally, Jessica has completed various business programs for the development of her companies.

MONICA ADWANI

"As Latino(a)s we tend to try to fit that box, but there is no shame in being ourselves."

For fifteen years, I felt trapped in a box within my industry. I was doing what others told me to do, trying to fit in and cater to their expectations. Often feeling oppression and discrimination. Consistently trying to fit the mold, trying to get rid of my loud laugh, accent, and hiding my roots. I tried to cater to others' wants and needs because, after all, my success was dependent on being accepted and building relationships.

One day three years ago, something happened that changed everything. It was during a conversation over un café that made me realize I wasn't letting myself be more than what others wanted me to be I helped everyone else succeed but me. For a very long time I was told I couldn't, I was too expensive, I needed to tone it down, I needed to wait, I wasn't allowed to cater to THOSE people, meaning people like that look, sound, and acted like me.

As a woman and Latina in a white male-dominated industry, I felt like I was being pushed down and not allowed to fully tap into my potential, I lost my identity. It took me fifteen years to realize it.

What started as a casual conversation with a good friend and potential business partner turned into clarity, and the biggest AHA! moment in my life. After that café, my vision for serving our underserved community became clear. We talked about the challenges we faced and how we could work together to make a difference. I realized that by showing up for others and working together, we could grow, succeed, and bridge a gap not just for consumers, but employees, women, and people who were facing the same issues as me.

Today, I help women step into their power, happily servicing our community owning one of the most successful Latino Insurance lead brokerages in America. I have the ability to walk into rooms and change lives by sharing my truth, recognizing that opening doors, creating connections, and being a servant leader is my superpower. I am not ashamed to be Latina, a human who makes mistakes daily, but who is fighting for a future of equity, inclusion, and diversification.

It's my goal to help our community understand that we are the only ones responsible for holding back and that we should and could achieve our highest potential. We need to believe in ourselves and our ability to break barriers and create new paths. We can't continue to close our own doors, because together, we can create a better world for ourselves and future generations. It's our responsibility to build the bridge and stepping stones to create generational wealth and eliminate the discrimination that happens in the workplace and towards consumers. We are PEOPLE, just like anyone else: capable, educated, hungry, dynamic and, above all, deserving.

BIOGRAPHY

Monica Adwani was born and raised in Puerto Rico and completed multiple degrees in Information Management, Medical Coding, and Business Management from the InterAmerican University of Puerto Rico. She then moved to Massachusetts and completed studies at Fisher College in Boston. Monica's education and curious mind are the catalysts that opened the doors to the insurance industry, leadership, and community building. Committed to growth, innovation, and transformation, she continues to drive significant impact by changing the way we think and perform by fostering inclusivity and diversification. Monica wants to help build a bridge for individuals to lead, to manage and to operate differently.

REPRESENTING VULNERABLE
COMMUNITIES AND BREAKING
DOWN GENERATIONAL BARRIERS

MARIA AGUILAR-ROCHA

"The road to achieving your dreams and excelling in your profession may be difficult for a first-generation person, but the privilege to represent vulnerable communities and the opportunity to break down generational barriers will serve as the fuel that keeps you moving forward."

Being born to low-income, Spanish-speaking, Mexican immigrant parents with only an elementary school education, the probability that I would attend a top law school and become an attorney seemed fairly unlikely. But it proved to be the very circumstance that shaped me into the person I am and the profession I chose to pursue.

For those who are children of immigrants, it will not be shocking if you served as an interpreter and translator, bargaining agent, and sometimes even legal advocate, all during your childhood years. My experience was no different. My parents spoke only Spanish when they arrived in the United States, and while they labored to remain within Spanish-speaking circles, that was not always possible. A phone call or interaction in English sparked tremendous anxiety in them, and they often rushed for my assistance. At an early age, I learned to be their representative in uncomfortable situations. It was a role that I cherished because of the impact I realized I could have on their lives. From then on, I became obsessed with being the best advocate I could be for them and others in similar circumstances.

A pivotal moment that put me on the trajectory toward becoming an attorney occurred when I was in middle school. A former teacher who also taught a legal studies elective course asked me if I would be interested in joining the class. Until then, although I was passionate about advocacy, I had not considered a career in law. At that time, no one in my family had attended college—definitely not law school—and I barely knew what an attorney did. But everything changed once I joined the class and was chosen to be a trial attorney in a mock trial competition. As I sifted through the evidence, examined the witnesses, and delivered my arguments, I realized that becoming an attorney was exactly what I wanted to do. It was the profession that would provide me with the best skill set and platform to advocate for vulnerable communities and bring about much-needed change.

Through intense hard work, determination, and perseverance, I ultimately attended and graduated from Georgetown Law with a

Juris Doctor degree and Master of Laws in Securities and Financial Regulation. As an attorney, I have been able to work on a wide range of cases impacting vulnerable communities across the United States and abroad, including victims of financial fraud, immigrant families facing deportation, and indigent persons combating the criminal justice system. As challenging as the profession of attorney can be, it has been the most rewarding experience due to the impact of my work on marginalized people and the ability to influence the development of the law in a manner that is more just and equitable.

The road to achieving your dreams and excelling in your profession may be difficult for a first-generation person, but the privilege to represent vulnerable communities and the opportunity to break down generational barriers will serve as the fuel that keeps you moving forward.

BIOGRAPHY

Maria Aguilar-Rocha is an Attorney-Advisor at the Commodity Futures Trading Commission (CFTC), a United States government agency responsible for regulating the derivatives markets. She previously worked at the United States Department of Justice, handling high-profile cases involving financial crimes, and the law firms of Katten Muchin Rosenman LLP and Baker Botts LLP, handling complex litigation and compliance matters. Maria received a Juris Doctor degree and a Master of Laws in Securities and Financial Regulation from Georgetown Law and a Bachelor's Degree in Political Science from the University of California, Los Angeles. She has spearheaded numerous diversity, equity and inclusion efforts.

MAKING A CHANGE THROUGH MUSIC

SOPHIA ANGELICA

"If you have a passion and a talent for something, use it for good."

An overcrowded audience cheered as an overwhelming energy bounced off the walls of the auditorium. At the end of the performance, groups of students stood to meet me, waiting in a line that extended outside the university. Later, I laid back on a high-speed train on the way back to Taipei, processing this life-changing moment in time.

When Simone, Director of Youth for Human Rights Taiwan, had invited me to her country to do a university tour in March 2018, I didn't quite know what to expect. The organization puts together a university tour every year, inviting international activists to uplift students all around the country. My job was to perform my own music and speak about human rights, which I had just done at university No. 4.

Simone was sitting next to me, reading the surveys the students filled out about their reactions to the presentation. Many described an urge to follow their dreams, reduce bullying, and advocate for human rights in their own communities. Then, Simone pulled one out that shocked me. It said, "Now I realize I shouldn't commit suicide."

That is when I registered the effect that music can have on one life, including my own. My journey towards using music as activism began at a young age. Singing at a family party was the one moment that changed everything, when Dr. Judy Kuriansky, the head of the Mental Health NGO for the United Nations (UN), approached me and said, "You have to sing at the United Nations!" She essentially led me into a parallel universe, one that would then become my life.

I soon was performing at a variety of conferences and sections of the UN that can hold thousands of people at the age of fourteen. I learned about the thirty human rights, among them one that resonated with me, "No discrimination."

As a Hispanic with light skin, I constantly get asked why I'm not dark-skinned or how I can speak Spanish.

I couldn't understand the stereotypes or how people can be treated with such animosity just for being who they are. However, I always said that if you have a passion and a talent for something, to use it for good. That became my mission through music, and that is the message I wanted these students to take away with them in Taiwan.

The final stop after the fourteen universities we visited was the 6th Asia-Pacific Human Rights Summit. I could never forget the kindness I experienced, the young volunteers of the summit sharing the beauty of their country and friendship with me.

The end of my trip near, I sat in the back of a conference

room, listening to the volunteers go up one by one with their final statements. A young girl locked eyes with me, reading a bittersweet goodbye.

She ended with another one of those statements you have to process before reacting.

"I want to be the Taiwanese version of Sophia. She inspired me."

At that moment, I knew this is what I was meant to do with my life. And it's just the beginning.

BIOGRAPHY

With her debut album "#Angelicas," talented Argentinean singer-songwriter Sophia Angelica has written and created an energy-infused, emotional roller coaster. Having performed around the world as a global human rights activist, she also works closely with the UN. In 2018, Sophia went on a University Human Rights Tour in Taiwan. She has received the HOLA Breakthrough Artist Award, the Presidential Volunteer Service Award, and a Marvin Hamlisch International Music Award under Contemporary Pop, presented by Clive Davis. Having just returned from being invited by the Gates Foundation to perform in Thailand, Sophia continues to sing in well-known venues, such as Birdland Jazz Club, Times Square, and Yankee Stadium.

MATILDE ARREGUIN

*"My experiences brought their own set of challenges, but they
also gave me the strength, motivation, and resilience to succeed."*

Growing up low income had become a way of life for my family. My parents worked tirelessly to make ends meet, but it never seemed to be enough. We lived in a one-bedroom apartment in the suburbs of Chicago, sharing a single bedroom amongst the five of us.

My parents, being immigrants, faced additional challenges because of their status. They had to take any job that they could, often low paying. After the birth of my third sibling, my mother faced several health issues that left her unable to return to work, which put a massive strain on our family's finances. My parents could no longer keep up with mortgage payments and we were forced to leave our home. Despite losing everything and becoming homeless, my parents tried to stay positive and continued looking for work. We relocated to a different state, where family members took us in until my parents were able to get back on their feet. After some time, my parents found jobs that allowed us to get a small place for our now family of six, a place we could call home again.

Despite the financial struggles, I was determined to succeed. I knew that education was my ticket out of poverty. As a first-generation student, however, there was a lack of guidance and support in navigating the college education system. My parents did not have the knowledge or experience to help me understand the intricacies of the college application process. I felt like I was at a disadvantage from my peers, having to figure it out on my own and often finding myself feeling lost and overwhelmed. Nevertheless, I was extremely fortunate to have some incredible mentors in my life who saw potential in me and encouraged me to keep pushing forward. There were teachers, coaches, and community leaders who went above and beyond to support me. Through their guidance and support, I was able to secure scholarships that covered my expenses during all four years of undergrad at Iowa State University.

A few years after completing my undergrad, I yearned for work that would be more impactful. I continued my studies at Wake Forest University in Winston-Salem, North Carolina, and completed a graduate degree in law. I transitioned into an equal opportunity compliance role that allowed me to take my unique perspective, experience, and deep understanding of social issues to push for positive change and greater equality.

Being low-income, daughter of undocumented immigrants, and a first-generation student, never did I imagine myself to be in the position I am fortunate to be in today. My experiences brought their own set of challenges, but they also gave me the strength, motivation, and resilience to succeed. I am proud of my background and the unique perspectives it has given me. I am determined to make the most out of the opportunities I have been given. I hope that my story can inspire others who are facing similar challenges to persevere and pursue their dreams.

BIOGRAPHY

Matilde Arreguin is a Diversity and Equal Opportunity Compliance Professional currently at IBM. She holds a Bachelor of Science from Iowa State University in Ames, Iowa, and a Master of Studies in Law from Wake Forest University. In the face of adversity, Matilde embraced challenging experiences and turned any setback into an opportunity. From an early age, Matilde recognized the immense impact individuals can have when they support one another. Inspired by the kindness and support she received from her community, Matilde has devoted her time to giving back to the community and embraces the opportunity to make a positive difference.

IF YOU DON'T BELIEVE IN YOURSELF, WHO WILL?

RITA BAUTISTA

"If you align your mind and heart, and you're truly connected to what you're passionate about, you can endure just about anything and come out on the other side."

When the pandemic hit, I worked in medical sales and often visited doctors at Houston Medical Center, the largest medical center in the world. I walked in one Monday, and it was so quiet you could hear a pin drop. It felt like when hurricane Katrina hit New Orleans—a hush, an odd calm before the storm.

The company I worked for was insensitive to the shutdowns happening everywhere, and they acted like COVID-19 was no big deal. I think they expected to make a huge profit during that time and didn't appreciate how vocal I became, questioning the safety of continuing "business as usual."

In the end, we went remote. They had trackers on our phones and fired me for traveling to Chicago, even though my phone records proved I called 40 offices and put in a full day working.

Despite working for them for two years and selling $2 million in product, I received no notice or severance. I was angry at the unfairness of it, especially since the owner had been a friend.

My savings didn't last as long as I'd hoped, and I found myself having to apply for rental assistance and food stamps while deciding what to do next. Should I look for a new sales job? Or was there something else for me?

A few months before, I had started a podcast, "Empowerment and All That," as a hobby so I could interview people and share empowering stories with the world.

I realized there was a lack of representation in podcasting—I couldn't find other people that looked like me. So, I decided to create it, and that's when Latina Podcasters was born.

It started as a Facebook group with the hope of connecting to other Latina podcasters, and almost overnight, 700 people signed up. Then, right when I lost my job, this group attracted the attention of Denise Soler Cox, the founder of Project Eñye in Denver, Colorado.

She gave me a scholarship for her new accelerator program to help people build a business from a dream or idea, which helped kick the growth of Latina Podcasters into high gear. I started to develop the structure and then built it out, announcing that we would become a network in 2021.

Our revenue comes from the sale of ads. I knew if I could sell medical products I didn't care about, I could easily sell ads for a network that was my heart, and I was able to take the Latina Podcaster network to over $1 million in revenue in under two years.

One of the most powerful things we have in this world is an idea. Ideas can build empires or break people down. They can be destructive or become a revolution in our experience as humans. So, why not take a chance on my idea, on me?

I know now that you can't get from one place to another without a strong network of really engaged people, and I'm lucky to be part of that.

BIOGRAPHY

Rita Bautista is passionate about elevating cultura and inspiring others. This first-generation American, born to Honduran parents, founded the Latina Podcasters in 2019 as a way for big brands to reach first-generation US Hispanics and the Latinx community through the authentic voices of podcasters. As a part of this effort, Rita founded the Latina Podcasters Network and Latino Pods and has worked extensively for more than a decade, representing the Latinx culture in education, government, business, and sports. She also enjoys being outdoors while teaching classes as a certified yoga instructor.

FROM DOUBT TO MASTERPIECE: A STORY OF RESILIENCE

ANDERSON BETANCOURT

"Embracing the unknown is like opening the door to endless possibilities, where courage intertwines with curiosity, and the extraordinary awaits your arrival."

Embrace the unknown. "Every stroke of color on the sculptures and canvas is a testament to my journey of self-discovery and resilience. Embracing the unknown led me to a door full of possibilities," I whispered to myself, as if reaffirming my commitment to the path I had chosen.

I remember the day I set foot in New York City, leaving behind Caracas, Venezuela. I remember standing on a rooftop in Brooklyn, with tears in my eyes and a mix of fear and excitement in my heart. Taking a deep breath, I said to myself, "New York, you are so pretty and so huge, but you are not trying to scare me. I am the one who is intimidated by you. Let's make a deal. I am going to embrace the unknown, but you are going to walk alongside me and show me what you have."

Those words opened up my mind and recalibrated my mindset. I realized that to unleash the power within us, we have to go for it fearlessly, and that if you encounter a rock on your way, just make a sculpture out of it. At that moment I started working on a collection that had given me so much, The Royal Blue Collection. It came from my desire to connect our real world, society, and nature with human feelings. The pieces of this collection symbolize loyalty, truthfulness, harmony, wisdom, tolerance, serenity, honesty, freedom, and happiness—qualities that we as human beings strive for.

At some point I stopped working with my art because I was affected by being in a different country. But then one night, I got up in the middle of the night praying and these words came to me, "Consistency determines your future not your desire, Anderson." Next day, I went back to work and kept going until I finished.

Through the highs and lows, I discovered the transformative power of embracing vulnerability. I allowed myself to be open to new experiences, even when they felt uncomfortable. It was through these moments of discomfort that I experienced the most significant personal and artistic growth.

As I settled into my new life, the vast artistic tapestry of New York became my inspiration and playground. I immersed myself in the art scene, attended galleries, explored museums, and connected with fellow artists. Each encounter and experience shaped my perspective and expanded the horizons of my creativity.

But amidst the breathtaking exhibitions and cultural richness, I faced moments of self-doubt. The competitive nature of the art world and the constant comparison to other talented individuals tested my resilience. However, I refused to let these challenges dampen my spirit. I recognized that my journey was unique, and it was essential to embrace my own artistic voice.

As I look back on my journey, I realize that embracing change and self-discovery are the fundamental lessons I've learned as an artist. My artwork has become my sanctuary, a space where I can freely express myself and capture the essence of the world around me.

"Embracing the unknown is like opening the door to endless possibilities, where courage intertwines with curiosity, and the extraordinary awaits your arrival."

BIOGRAPHY

Anderson Betancourt is a Venezuelan-born artist based in New York City. With a background in social communication and cosmetology, he discovered his passion for art and embarked on a creative journey. He launched his online Art Gallery www. artebamart.com. Focusing on painting and sculpture, Anderson's work reflects his imaginative spirit and unique perspective. His artistic vision shines through in his captivating Royal Blue Collection, featuring limited edition pieces with striking and asymmetric designs. With a commitment to pushing artistic boundaries, Anderson's art captivates viewers and invites them into his imaginative world. As a promising talent in the New York art scene, he continues to inspire with his visually compelling and thought-provoking creations.

GUT FEELINGS LEAD YOU TO THE
MOST UNEXPECTED PLACES

MARIANA CANTÚ

"Every prescription only fits one vision and those who fail sometimes do not realize how close they were to succeeding. I was about to reject producing the film; thankfully, I had a gut feeling."

As children, we all have dreams of someday becoming an astronaut, a doctor, a scientist, etc. The only thing I knew at that age was that I wanted to be surrounded by beauty.

My life has revolved around doctors since I was seven years old because I was diagnosed with Hashimoto. At that time, I felt a sense of embarrassment around my diagnosis because other kids seemed healthy. So, my parent's way of making me feel better after any doctor's appointment was to take me shopping.

I will never forget when I was twelve years old I saw my first couture dress, a red Valentino gown. I vividly remember all the hand-embroidered details. In that moment, I knew my life passion was in fashion. I was going against all odds and I would repeatedly get comments like, "You're never going to get paid much if you study Fashion."

I decided to enroll in business school, mostly to please those around me. But I started missing classes and sometimes I wouldn't come home to sleep and lied about what I was doing. The truth is, I was sleeping over at a seamstress' house designing and creating my portfolio to fashion school.

Three rejected applications later, I finally got accepted by the Fashion Institute of Technology. Fast-forward, I got hired to be a producer by Italian Vogue as my first job out of college. Eventually, Italian Vogue closed its offices in New York City and I was left without a job. But I had a gut feeling and saw it as an opportunity. A year later, I had my own production agency, MC Colectiva, LLC. I was working with other international publications and some of the world's top photographers, models, and stylists. It was a dream come true.

A few years later, COVID-19 happened and, unfortunately, the agency was not doing well. I was on the verge of giving up. A year later, I got a call to produce a short film for a friend. We had only two weeks to prep, and I was unsure of doing it because I knew a lot of things could go badly with such short prep time. There was something I loved so much about the project though, maybe it was the young director's passion and energy, it resembled mine a few years back. I had another gut feeling to take it and go all in. Alongside Director and Co-producer Matias Figueroa, we produced a short film in 2021 with many mistakes in the middle of a pandemic, and yet we persevered. There was passion and drive, and neither of us has let any of our childhood dreams go.

Recently I received the most unexpected and exciting news on one of the projects I produced, and I'm just getting started on the rest. Things might take time, but if you believe, and never surrender to those dreams, then they will be yours. Every prescription only fits one vision and those who fail sometimes do not realize how close they were to succeeding. I was about to reject producing the film; thankfully, I had a gut feeling.

BIOGRAPHY

Originally from Mexico, New York-based producer Mariana Cantú, is a well-versed fashion aficionado, who began her fashion career from working at Harper's Bazaar to publishing high profile Vogue Italia editorials. She found her passion in the editorial field, while previously working for other publications to then starting her own production agency, MC Colectiva, where she produces and consults for several brands. Mariana's most recent work includes being the VIP and Panelists Director for the Latin American Fashion Summit, producing an Academy Award Short Film contender called "Dimensions of Self," and working as a Marketing Director for Faith Connexion.

FROM FLAG ASSISTANT TO GLOBAL LEADER: A JOURNEY OF PERSEVERANCE, COURAGE, AND GROWTH MINDSET

ULLISSES CARUSO

"Nothing good comes easy. Keep pushing forward, keep striving for that dream, and I promise the good will come your way."

I was just fourteen years old when the realization hit me like a ton of bricks—what would I do when my parents were no longer around? We were a middle-class family in Brazil, and while I had a comfortable life, I knew that their income would never be enough to sponsor my college. So, I decided that I needed to start working soon to secure my future.

I found my first job as a flag assistant at an indoor karting arena at the age of fifteen. Despite the criticisms of my friends and relatives, I felt a sense of fulfillment that I had never experienced before. Bringing my first salary home to my mother and seeing the pride in her eyes was one of the best moments of my life.

By age twenty, I was working as Coordinator at a computing

science school with a promising career path ahead, but I still felt unfulfilled. That's when I decided to sell my motorcycle to embark on a two-year backpacking trip to London. The experience helped me to grow as a person in ways I could never have imagined. When I returned to Brazil, I faced the challenge of finding a job that would leverage my newfound language skills without a degree or technical background. Then, I heard about IBM hiring employees with English as a second language. To my surprise, I was offered a junior position, which allowed me to get my foot in the door.

For the next four years, I worked full-time at IBM and studied in the mornings to earn my Bachelor's degree. The hard work paid off when I was promoted to my first management position. I continued to take on new challenges and roles in Brazil, eventually leading operations and financials for a 1,000-person organization. I earned Supply Chain and Agile Certificates and even won two innovation awards.

My success caught the attention of IBM's global leadership team, and I was offered a position as a second-line manager in the Philippines. There, I implemented Agile practices and eliminated 30,000 hours of manual work through innovation and process optimization. When my time in the Philippines ended, I received a pro bono assignment in India, supporting an HIV Association. This experience showed me the importance of giving back, humility, and compassion.

Eventually, I went to the United States (US), where I currently lead the Strategy and Client Advocacy for shared services. In this role, I have been able to lead Innovation Programs, formulate strategies, and deploy a client advocacy program. These actions have been recognized through three industry awards which I share with my team and all the supporters who believe in me.

I could not have achieved all that I have without the support of my husband, who lives with me in the US, along with our two cats. As a Latino/Hispanic and gay man working in the US, I am incredibly proud of my journey and the diversity, perseverance, and courage it represents.

BIOGRAPHY

Ullisses Caruso's story is a testament to determination and courage against all odds. Born in a middle-class family in Brazil, without a Bachelor's Degree and technical background, he started as a junior at IBM, and today he is a successful Strategy and Operations leader. With nineteen years of experience, he has managed a large organization in the Philippines and achieved several milestones, including Agile and Client Advocacy program implementation, two innovation awards, two Grand Stevie Awards, and a pro bono assignment in India. He lives in the US with his husband and two cats and proud of his diversity and experiences.

LIVING WITH ZERO REGRETS

MELISSA CASEY-WOODCOCK

"I now make it a priority to think big, imagine the possibilities, and take risks."

A few years ago, I got the push to live my life with zero regrets. It started as an exciting conversation about career progression that I had desperately been waiting for after many years of hard work and determination. I was told I was being considered for two executive roles and that I would get to pick my choice. Two weeks later, the rug was pulled from under my feet as I was told that I could no longer be considered for an executive role at all and possibly not in the future. I was disappointed, sad, angry, and confused all at once.

I told myself that I had three choices: 1) stay on my path and keep hoping for a change, 2) leave the company and pursue progression elsewhere, or 3) stay and push myself to transform in ways that I had never done before. I didn't have the answers then, but I knew the same path wouldn't work and leaving the company would just be taking the easy way out. I started my journey by writing my first book, which I used as a guide to coach myself through reflection on what I really wanted to get out of life. I went on to consider work possibilities that I had never imagined and also took bigger risks like competing in a company-wide contest where my idea won second place. Now, I'm pushing my limits by pursuing a PhD in Psychology. I could not have gotten through that experience without my husband, who was incredibly supportive in giving me the space and time I needed to reflect and focus. Separately, I am very thankful to my management team, which demonstrated honesty and transparency while supporting me, even if they couldn't control the obstacles and uncertainty that I faced in my career progression.

The most significant gifts I got from this experience came from within, where I found my passion and voice. I am an introvert at heart, and speaking up and leading amongst other highly talented leaders hasn't always come naturally. This experience pushed me outside of my comfort zone to realize where I can add value to others. Eventually, my risks paid off, and I finally progressed to the executive ranks. However, what I learned from pushing myself is far greater than any promotion can give me. I am no longer too shy to speak up for what I believe in or too busy to follow my dreams. I now make it a priority to think big, imagine the possibilities, and take risks. My dream is to help others achieve their dreams and live with zero regrets, no matter their challenges.

BIOGRAPHY

Melissa Casey-Woodcock is a certified life coach, author, and Human Resources (HR) professional with a passion for learning and development and talent management. Melissa has nineteen years of experience in HR and is currently leading talent management processes for about 18,000 professionals in PepsiCo. She published Zero Regrets in 2019 as a coaching guide to help individuals lead a better quality of life. Melissa's learning and development work has won seven external excellence awards between 2017-2020. Melissa has a Master's Degree in Entrepreneurship from Southern Methodist University (SMU), a Bachelor's Degree in Business from the University of Michigan, and is currently pursuing a PhD in Industrial and organizational (I/O) Psychology.

MIGUEL CASTILLO

"¿Mijo, qué quieres ser cuando seas grande?" I responded. "Papa, quiero ser astronauta y ir a las estrellas."

"¿Mijo, qué quieres ser cuando seas grande?" I responded. "Papa, quiero ser astronauta y ir a las estrellas." The year was 1973 and my dad was looking at the moon and stars with his usual curiosity every time he would enjoy a beer. He joined the Mexican Military in 1957 with hopes of getting a college degree.

I remember "boleando zapatos" when I was seven year old on the border, working on the international bridge and finding recycled items at the city dump to resell. Back then I didn't know I was poor as I had fun with my brothers, rode "el camion" and immersed myself reading comic books. Sometimes we would wait for my mom to cross the bridge with treats for us from the United States' side. I didn't celebrate Christmas, but I celebrated Dia de Los Reyes Magos as I anxiously awaited a peso or two with mints inside our shoes every January 6. The best present ever was my family after my dad returned from the US as he worked in the fields, construction, and other jobs to support our family.

For the first time, I felt fear as my family was separated to make the journey north in 1979. First my brothers, then my parents and younger siblings. I stayed behind with my sister, who worked as a maid at a ranch. She was thirteen years old and I was nine. I cried, blamed my sister, didn't want to go to school, but found purpose in reading. Living in a small RV with no electricity, no water, cold, and no snacks at night. To keep my mind occupied from sadness of not seeing my family, I would immerse myself in reading comic books. In my imagination, I was the superhero who would bring my family together again.

In the summer of 1980, we took the underground road hacia el norte. As I got out of the bus station at night, I ran as fast as I could and hugged my brother, Andy, and the rest of my family, crying with joy as I saw them again. This is one of the best moments of my life. As we settled in the US, we became migrant farmworkers, struggled, faced challenges, and discrimination but always remained together.

In 1993, I graduated from college. First one in my family. I felt the same as the young boy working on the streets "boleando zapatos." I saw my dad and mom with teary eyes as I hugged them dressed with my cap and gown. My dad said, "Mijo, gracias por terminar, cambiaste tu futuro y ahora empieza tu camino." The Pandemic of 2020 took my inspiration in front of my eyes. Seeing my dad lying on a bed through a camera taking his last breaths. Not being able to hug him, comfort him, or hear his "consejos" one last time. After all these years, I finally realized that his journey was my journey. Esto es para ti papá.

BIOGRAPHY

Miguel Castillo is an Executive Director of Schools, a former school principal and math teacher. He began his education career twenty-nine years ago. His passion is serving underprivileged, underserved, and historically marginalized students of color and communities. His work in school improvement led to his school being named one of the best schools in Texas and California and was featured on the front page of the New York Times and national news network Univision. An immigrant and former migrant farmworker, Miguel believes in providing the same equal opportunities he had to struggling students for a chance at a better life.

THE SUNSHINE BEHIND THE DARK CLOUD

TARA CLAUDIO-RIVERA

"I was stronger than I knew and just had to find that rainbow behind the dark clouds."

I was running as fast as I could and no matter how fast I kept running I was not moving. I kept asking for help, but the words were not coming out; and the more I tried to speak, the less I was being heard. I kept running, but I was running out of time because the footsteps kept getting closer and closer. All I could hear was my mom calling me "Mama, Mama" in Spanish; and at that moment, I woke up screaming for my mom and I cried myself to sleep again.

I can recall from a very young age that despite having a smile on my face there was this emptiness and sadness that I carried wherever I went. My mom was in an abusive relationship with my dad for many years and when he passed away, I did not know whether to cry, feel sad, or relieved. We were at peace or at least that is what I was hoping for. My family and I faced some difficult, unforeseen circumstances after his passing. Throughout my childhood, I shared a twin bed with my younger brother in a small room that we could barely walk in. There was a small window no kitchen or bathroom—it felt like a jail cell. We shared a first-floor bathroom with four other strangers—two of them were males who used drugs intravenously. Crack was big during that era and the different color tops were found in the shower and floor. I would hold my brother's hand tight as my mom cleaned the entire bathroom with Clorox and when it was cleaned, we quickly jumped in and out making sure we reached the important parts. I was so afraid at times that I wished I could have crawled into a hole, hide, and never come out. That was not possible, so I focused on school, because I knew there was something better waiting for me. My mother and brother were my motivation. I was determined to not continue to live in poverty. We were placed in a shelter and then had our own apartment. That experience stood with me my entire life, but I refused for it to determine by destiny.

Looking back at my childhood, I did not know where my next meal was going to come from. But I knew where I was heading. There was nothing that was going to stand in my way. My childhood experience taught me the meaning of never giving up despite whatever obstacles were put in front of me. Despite my upbringing, I was able to overcome my fears and I realized I was stronger than I knew and just had to find that rainbow behind the dark clouds. I went on to finish school and obtained two Master's Degree. I was able to look for the sun after the rain and the stars when it was dark.

BIOGRAPHY

Tara Claudio-Rivera was born and raised in Brooklyn, New York. Her mom was from Ponce and her father was from a little town called Catano, Puerto Rico. Tara is married and has a seventeen-year-old son and thirteen-year-old daughter. They moved to North Carolina five years ago and reside in Apex, North Carolina. She has a Bachelor's Degree in Psychology, a Master's Degree in Social Work, and a second Master's Degree in Education General and Special Education for grades one through six. She is the middle child, has a half-brother and lost her younger brother five months ago. Tara enjoys spending time with her family and watching her daughter play soccer and her son play football.

RAUL CONTRERAS

"A river finds its course no matter how many barricades and obstacles it encounters. It creates new paths. It adapts. It's flexible with its environment. A river doesn't know exactly where it will end up, but each new direction it takes creates a perfect, unique path."

On a warm June day in 2019, after cleaning my friend's apartment to make ends meet, I was riding the M102 bus home to Harlem, when I received the following email:

Hi Raul,

Hope you had a nice weekend. Our team would love to have you join West Side Story as an offstage Shark swing. However, since you are in the United States on an O-1 visa, rather than a Green Card, Actors Equity needs to approve the casting decision, since it would technically be an alien taking the job . . .

You can imagine my excitement—after a long audition process, I was just offered a position on Broadway! I wanted to scream the big news to the whole bus, but the last line of the email made me keep my screams (and my celebration) to myself.

An "alien taking the job?"

I'd only been in New York City for one year, and all the immigration stuff was still very new to me. But I knew this was going to cause some trouble.

The following month, I had surgery on my leg. As a starving artist, I decided to return to Mexico, instead of staying in New York City, where it costs money even to breathe. I would stay in my hometown of Monterrey to complete my mandatory three months of post-op rest, and then return to the city for my big, Broadway debut.

While in Mexico, I received an email from the casting office, telling me that the conversations around casting an "alien" in the show were happening, and that the West Side Story team was really fighting the union to have me in the show. But time passed and passed, and right before we were supposed to start rehearsals, I received a phone call from one of the producers, saying they did everything they could but the union's final response was "No."

I was devastated. Even with an O-1 visa—which was incredibly hard to get, by the way—I was still having to deal with all these limitations as a Mexican performer in America. This country, that once welcomed immigrants with open arms, was now creating all these laws and rules, making everything more and more difficult for us.

The following months in Monterrey were not easy: post-surgery, no job, and no plan to return to New York City. But against all odds, with the little money I'd managed to save, I finally made my way back to the city. I was ready to audition for everything, and knock down every door that stood in my way. And then . . .

February 2020.

Well, we know what happened next—a pandemic that stopped the world (and any chance of me making any money).

If it wasn't for the generosity of the people I was living with at the time, I wouldn't have been able to cover my rent or even buy groceries. I don't know how I got so lucky—my mom says it was God—and as the months passed, I was able to find things to do here and there to make some money of my own again.

I clung to the city (as we say in Mexico) "with teeth and nails."

After a year or so, as things began returning to "normal," I launched a crowdfunding campaign to pay for my new visa, and found a new theatrical agent. They sent me to my first audition since the pandemic, for a Broadway show called, *Moulin Rouge!*

Eight months later, I was offered an ensemble role in the show. And this time, the union was on my side. After the pandemic (and because of some new perspectives on diversity and racial equality), Actor's Equity changed their rules—O-1 visa holders were finally going to be able to take Broadway contracts.

It's been almost two years since I joined the cast of *Moulin Rouge!* and I can't say it's been easy. In fact, it's been one of the most challenging chapters of my life. But I couldn't be more grateful to doing what I'm doing, and I'm so proud of what I've accomplished.

When I reflect on my journey so far, I can't help but think of a river: facing obstacles, forging new paths, adapting to its surrounding, constantly changing course . . .

But always finding its way.

BIOGRAPHY

Originally from Monterrey, Mexico, Raúl Contreras is a queer performer and choreographer currently a swing, Dance Captain and Santiago U/S at *Moulin Rouge! The Musical* on Broadway. He previously danced for Ballet Metropolitano de Monterrey, Metamorphosis Dance Collective and Ballet Hispánico. He is a graduate of the Escuela Superior de Música y Danza de Monterrey with a Bachelor of Fine Arts (BFA) in Contemporary Dance. He has served as a teacher, choreographer, and artistic director for Universidad de Monterrey's Dance Group, winning several dance competitions in Mexico and the United States. He has danced pieces from renowned choreographers, such as Anabelle Lopez Ochoa, Gustavo Ramírez Sansano, Iratxe Ansa, Edgar Zendejas, and Tania Perez Salas, among others.

FROM A HOMEMADE SATELLITE DISH TO EMPOWERING HISPANICS THROUGH TECHNOLOGY EDUCATION

ARIEL CORO

"I always remember my mission to educate Latinos to embrace tech. It saved my life, and I know it can propel our community to unprecedented success."

Growing up in Cuba during the 1990s, I learned early the power of curiosity and invention when resources are limited. I thought I had a normal childhood, but living in a communist country traumatized my life. I'll never forget one day in fifth grade, I was forced to stand alone in the school courtyard facing the students, having to "confess" publicly why I wasn't good enough to participate in an after-school education program for "good communist-compliant students." Instead, I was sent to a government center fixing electronics and telephone systems as a punishment. On that day, I felt hopeless because I was led to believe that if I didn't comply with the doctrine, I wasn't going to have a future. What I didn't realize then is that what felt like misfortune sent me on a triumphant path.

Since I was a kid, I was fascinated with technology, a love that I picked up from my father, who was a ham (amateur) radio operator and was always tinkering with electronics. This curiosity took me places. Living through the Cuban "Período Especial" economic crisis in the early 1990s, I built a homemade satellite dish from parts of an old Soviet radio, a coffee can, a mosquito net, and some other discarded electronic components. We now were able to watch "forbidden" TV channels, such as CNN, allowed only for the island's tourists and elite government officials. This newly found access to information transformed my life by opening a window to the outside world, which eventually led me to escape Cuba at eighteen years old.

Arriving in the United States (US), barely able to speak English, didn't stop me. Freedom allowed me to build a career with self-taught tech skills. I started my own computer business and, a few years later, I was working for The Hubble Space Telescope, CheckPoint Software, and Cisco Systems as a Senior Cybersecurity Engineer consulting for some of the largest organizations in the world.

One day I was asked to comment in Spanish on Telemundo's national morning show about Identity theft, a new concept back then. After that interview, the calls kept coming, and eventually, I left Cisco to pursue a new career in media. Shortly after, Univision called, and I became the tech expert for Despierta America, the Number One morning show in Spanish in the US. I've done hundreds of radio and TV segments and used the media as a giant classroom to educate Hispanics on the importance of embracing technology and, ironically enough, I've been invited several times to comment about tech trends by CNN, the same "forbidden" channel that I watched while in Cuba hoping for a better future.

Fast forward a few years, I have launched a few companies, published a book, and have keynoted for some of the largest and most prestigious companies and educational institutions in the world, but I always remember my mission to educate Latinos to embrace tech. It saved my life, and I know it can propel our community to unprecedented success.

BIOGRAPHY

Ariel Coro is the premier tech expert and commentator for US Hispanic audiences. Acclaimed keynote speaker, media personality and author, Ariel's trailblazing career has propelled Hispanics in the US to embrace tech education for personal growth. His book, El Salto, published by Random House Vintage Español in 2012, offered Spanish speakers a fresh perspective and practical guide for living in the digital age while navigating the US. A small business owner, start-up co-founder, investor, and advisor to several Fortune 500 companies, today Ariel brings his innovation keynote speeches to mainstream by invigorating corporate diversity.

US NAVY SUBMARINE, AUTHOR,
GLOBAL CYBERSECURITY LEADER

ALFE CORONA

"You are more than a conqueror, and with God's help, you can achieve overwhelming victory."

Hello friends, I want to share with you a story of perseverance and success that comes from my personal experience.

As a member of the United States (US) Navy, I was part of the Gold Crew on the USS Maine SSBN 741, a multimillion-dollar nuclear missile submarine submerged deep in the Pacific Ocean. Our mission was to protect the US from enemy countries with nuclear weapons through strategic nuclear deterrence. It was a tough job, but I was proud to be part of such a critical mission.

In the control room, the atmosphere was tense, and everyone was quiet as we navigated the submarine through rough waters. As a top helm submarine driver, I was responsible for steering the ship, and I received recognition for my professionalism, leadership, and proficiency.

Despite being born and raised in the Dominican Republic, I became a US citizen and enlisted in the Navy, qualifying for submarines in just six months. It was a significant achievement that came with a lot of pressure. The Navy instills in us the importance of being qualified to save the ship from danger, flooding, fire, or to help fight against another ship or enemy submarine.

After serving for four years, I faced a dilemma. Should I re-enlist or become a civilian and pursue my college degrees? I chose the latter, and it was the best decision I ever made. I graduated with a Bachelor's Degree in Business and later earned a Master's Degree in Leadership and a Master's Degree in Cybersecurity from Fordham University in New York City.

But my journey wasn't always easy. Before joining the Navy, I struggled with low-paying jobs in New York City, where I was bullied on subway trains while studying and doing homework. I rented rooms and faced a low quality of life. But I believed in education and worked hard to become a successful person.

I attribute my success to my identity and the people I surround myself with. I always saw myself as more than a conqueror, and I surrounded myself with positive influences that helped me to achieve my goals. As the saying goes, "We are the five people we surround ourselves with," and I learned that by being selective with whom I spend time with, I can achieve great things.

Preparation for success takes effort and discipline, but it pays off. Now, as an author and successful cybersecurity professional, I can say that I started from the bottom, and now I'm here!

In conclusion, I want to share a message of hope and

encouragement with you. No matter where you come from or what challenges you face, never give up on your dreams. Surround yourself with positive influences, and believe in yourself. You are more than a conqueror, and with God's help, you can achieve overwhelming victory. As it says in Romans 8:37, "In all these things, we are more than conquerors through him who loved us."

Thank you for reading, and God bless you.

BIOGRAPHY

Alfe Corona, a bilingual Spanish immigrant from the Dominican Republic, has created a new life as a US citizen. With a strong work ethic and motivation, he served in the US Navy Submarines and holds multiple college degrees, including a Master of Science from Fordham University. Drawn to self-development books since childhood and inspired by the works of Paulo Coelho, Alfe has found his place in the literary world. In his professional career, he has excelled in leadership roles at reputable companies and is dedicated to assisting others in achieving the same success. As an author, his mission is to empower and inspire individuals to pursue their life goals by believing in their dreams and persevering.

REWRITING THE NARRATIVE

ELIZABETH CRUZ

"Embrace the power of our own narratives and let them serve as beacons of inspiration, resilience, and limitless possibilities for all."

Looking back at my childhood, I realize now that I was always a challenger of the status quo and stereotypes. Little did I know at the time that I was rewriting the narrative.

Born in Puerto Rico and growing up in Southbridge, Massachusetts, the youngest of eight, I faced many expectations and assumptions about what I should or shouldn't do. But I was determined to chart my own path and defy those limitations.

From a young age, I was quiet and an observer but with an adventurous spirit. I was always eager to learn and try new things that I felt added value, apply lessons learned from my mother and oldest sisters, becoming the first in my family to accomplish various milestones. I remember being the first one to learn how to drive a stick shift car, feeling a sense of empowerment as I conquered the open road because "mujeres" don't drive those types of cars let alone a Latina.

Breaking barriers seemed to be ingrained in my DNA. I ventured into the field of computer science, becoming the first in my family to graduate from college, achieving the remarkable distinction of graduating cum laude. It was a proud moment, not only for me but for my entire family. I knew it was a path less traveled by Latinas, but I was determined to excel. It wasn't easy being the only woman in my class, facing skepticism, and feeling like an outsider. The journey was filled with challenges, but I persevered, studying diligently and earning certifications from prestigious institutions, such as Clark University, Boston University, and Worcester Polytechnic Institute.

After working as senior software engineer and tech lead, I transitioned into an (information technology) IT consultant role for renowned companies, like Dell/EMC and Fidelity Investments, I actively engaged in community volunteering to share my experiences in the field of IT. During this time, I became increasingly aware of a disheartening trend among Latinx individuals, particularly Latinas. Many of them appeared disinterested in pursuing careers in technology, instead showing a preference for fields, such as social work, nursing, or human services. It became clear to me that there was a prevailing belief that one had to be exceptionally skilled in math or possess innate brilliance to succeed in the tech industry. Driven by a strong determination, I set out on a transformative journey to rewrite this narrative, establish myself as an example to inspire and empower girls, especially Latinas, to embrace science, technology, engineering and math (STEM) and not only to fearlessly challenge stereotypes, but also to demonstrate that nothing was beyond their reach when they wholeheartedly pursued their goals.

I want to share my story to inspire you to pursue your dreams and demonstrate that success isn't about conforming to societal expectations, but about embracing your passions and aspirations.

I believe that in order to bring about meaningful change, we must "Embrace the power of our own narratives and let them serve as beacons of inspiration, resilience, and limitless possibilities for all."

BIOGRAPHY

Elizabeth Cruz is a visionary leader in technology, real estate, and community advocacy, currently serving as the president of the Latin American Business Organization (LABO), which has a mission to increase Latin businesses' economic prosperity and business growth opportunities. As the CEO and owner of Cruz Realty Group with C21NE and Cruz Control Property Management, she has made significant strides in the world of real estate, assisting over 500 Hispanic families in achieving homeownership, entrepreneurship, and financial freedom. Elizabeth is the founder of Empowering Women Through Real Estate, a steering committee member of Unidos in Power, and board member of other non-profit organizations.

ERIC DI MONTE

"It is my hope if you are reading this and may be going through some challenges, that you continue to persevere. You will make it!"

Many times, we look at people and think or overlook where they came from and the challenges all of us go through in life, even thinking how "lucky" they are. People who have struggled and have overcome adversity know this to be mostly a misconception and luck has meant hard work to reach these goals.

To understand part of my journey, we go back in time when I grew up in a small town outside of Buenos Aires, Argentina, and my only language at home was Spanish. At the age of twelve, my family immigrated to Australia when it was the first time I was exposed to the English language. The challenge of being in a totally different country and culture and not being able to communicate was one of my earliest life challenges. An English/Spanish dictionary became my go-to lifesaver and it paid off, not only did I completed high school, I was the first in my family to graduate with a Bachelor's Degree.

In early 2001, having worked for several years and already married, my wife and I had just moved from Sydney, Australia, to New York to experience the American Dream. In that first year alone, we faced two major events: the tech bubble burst and 9/11. Regarding the latter event, I was working as a recruiter for a small downtown company and witnessed the Twin Towers at the World Trade Center collapse in front of me. Those days, weeks, and months that followed were filled with so many mixed emotions and self-doubts (similar for many). It would have been easier, safer, almost logical to go back . . . But, something kept pushing me to keep going, to persevere, and to not give up. We didn't want to look back (in this case, go back). There were many challenges that came by, but also many wonderful life-changing moments, such as the blessing of our first born.

Forward to 2008, the "worst financial crisis since The Great Depression" impacted multitudes of families, including myself. Weeks and months would pass by with little progress, the financial and personal impact affected my professional life and tested my limits. At that point, I knew a major change needed to take place and I had to reinvent myself. For the next four years (and still presently), I worked on expanding my professional connections with a focus on the Hispanic market. During those years (and landing interesting consulting roles along the way) I got more connected to people not only by networking, but also by connecting others. I gave without expecting anything in return and it would come back several times through the years.

Leading to the past decade, my perseverance and focus has

allowed me to work in roles where I have been "fortunate" to use my bilingual abilities in recruitment while growing professionally in managerial roles and responsibilities.

It is my hope, if you are reading this and may be going through some challenges, that you continue to persevere. You will make it! Sí, señor!

BIOGRAPHY

Eric Di Monte is well-known as a diligent bilingual networker and people connector. With proven years of experience in recruitment and diversity, equity and inclusion (DEI), he has worked on corporate and agency environments. His current role is Director of Talent Acquisition, and founder of the first Hispanic/Latin ERG at Warner Music Group. Previously, he was Talent Acquisition Manager at Univision, and has worked for companies, such as Verizon, PR Newswire, McGraw Hill, and Gartner. An established LinkedIn power user, he often is invited as guest speaker/panelist to present and train diverse audience groups. Eric has a Bachelor's Degree in Civil Engineering and is fully fluent in Spanish.

CELEBRATING LATINA SUCCESS
WITH THE ART REPRESENTATION

SANDRA LUCIA DIAZ

"Don't share your vision with people that don't have a vision."

I am Sandra Lucia Diaz a Colombian-American, the first in my family, living in Columbia, Maryland, with my husband and cats. My greatest passion is empowering women of color, first-generation Americans, and all women who strive to achieve their dreams, to feel valued and recognized for their accomplishments.

After losing my job at Amazon Prime Video, I sought therapy to cope with the sense of loss and confusion that came with losing a job that defined my identity. However, I soon realized that the corporate environment was not conducive to my personal growth, and the lack of representation in every industry I worked in motivated me to start my own company. I recognized that my dream was not to climb the corporate ladder, but rather a dream instilled in me by my parents.

I encourage you to reflect on your life and determine what you truly desire, rather than following what society or your family expects of you. After years of feeling like the token Latina in the beauty and tech industries, I realized that being laid off was the biggest blessing of my life. I implore you to ask yourself, What do you want to do, and who do you want to become?

During the pandemic, my husband and I moved to Maryland to be closer to his family. I used my first unemployment check to invest in a printer and start my entrepreneurship journey. With the help of mentors, like Marisol from Azteca Negra, I identified what I needed to focus on as a business owner and took my company to the next level. I reevaluated my friendships and contacts and spent time only with those who supported my journey. I stopped sharing my plans and began showing up as my authentic self. You are more than capable of anything you put your mind to; you are enough. This is your permission slip to pursue your dreams.

As the founder of Lucia Diaz, LLC, I strive to represent Afro Latinas and Latinas genuinely through personalized and thoughtful Latinx-inspired gifts. I launched the Graduation Card collection after realizing that big-box stores did not offer authentic Latinx representation. I am passionate about bringing Latinx representation to underrepresented industries by collaborating with luxury brands as a confident Latina and woman-owned business.

As a fashion illustrator, I work with visionary luxury brands to create impactful art that builds vibrant, long-lasting relationships with customers. My ultimate goal is to show people that their favorite brands understand them through personalized and thoughtful art that can move people and contribute to a greater cause.

BIOGRAPHY

Sandra Lucia Diaz is first generation Colombian-American and the Founder of Lucia Diaz, LLC, a Latina-owned business that empowers and honors Latinas through high-quality Illustrations. Lucia's artworks are created with the goal of providing cultural representation and pride so that mujeres poderosas, can see themselves represented in the world. https://shop.byluciadiaz.com/

WHEN FACED WITH A CHALLENGE, LOOK FOR THE SOLUTION

GINA DIAZ

"He then asked me the life-changing question. 'Would you rather be alive for three children or dead for four?'"

POP! That's the noise I heard and felt ripple through my body as I completed a set of crunches with my personal trainer. Little did I know that "POP" would change my life.

The pain was excruciating. My husband rushed me to the ER, where they told me I had a tumor in my left ovary that had ruptured. I was rushed into surgery and the last thing I remember is the worry on my husband's face.

The tumor was huge—five pounds—and just as my doctor told me post-surgery that preliminary testing determined it was cancer, I had an unsettling out-of-body experience. I sat, staring ahead, and I heard the machines buzzing as though my heartbeat had just flatlined.

At that moment, my mom, husband, and daughter walked in. They heard what she said, and immediately my mom started screaming and fainted. I snapped out of it but didn't have time to take in what the doctor had said because I was worried about my family.

It all hit me when I went to see my oncologist and read the words cancer unit. It was overwhelming and only got worse when I learned that I wouldn't be able to have any more children. I tried bargaining with the doctor to let me have one more child before removing the other ovary.

He then asked me the life-changing question. "Would you rather be alive for three children or dead for four?" I chose life, but I mourned the loss. Testing determined the cancer had not spread, so I didn't have to go through chemo or radiation. It was gone, and I was blessed to be cancer free.

Despite that, I became angry at God and life for taking away my ability to have more children, and it was then, at one of the most vulnerable times in my life, that my business partner nearly bankrupted me as well. I wasted almost a year before asking myself whether I wanted my legacy to be "Your mom became a drunk, angry person who lost it all," or if I wanted to find a solution to the challenge I faced.

I started thinking about my future, which led me to realize I had been living to work versus working to live. If something were to happen to me, what would be my legacy? What was my backup plan? What was my retirement? And that's when I decided to start investing in real estate.

The legal aspect of real estate investing is the biggest part of my business, and helping others learn how to invest and build their legacy is what makes me the happiest.

It has helped me to find a better work-life balance and I'm leaving a legacy for my kids, financially and personally. I have the respect and admiration of my kids, which is the most important to me, and if something were to happen to me tomorrow, I wouldn't be as afraid because I know they would be okay.

BIOGRAPHY

Gina Diaz has become one of the top immigration and real estate attorneys in Chicagoland. She opened Diaz Case Law to help immigrants find solutions to their difficulties. Her love for real estate investing added another dimension to her law practice as clients come to her for foreclosure defense, seeking ways to keep their homes, loan modifications, and short sales. Gina is known as the investor-approved #RightAttorney who assists other investors with difficult closings. She is also a founding member of We Win, LLC, an organization dedicated to introducing women to the world of real estate, and We Win, NFP.

RICARDO DIAZ

"If you love what you are doing, you will be successful."

My story is a common story among immigrants in El Paso. I had always dreamed of a better life. Born into poverty in the border city of El Paso, Texas, I faced numerous obstacles and hardships from an early age. Through luck or desperation, I happen to possess a relentless amount of determination to overcome my circumstances and forge a path towards success.

Growing up, I witnessed the struggles my parents faced as they worked tirelessly to make ends meet. Nothing came easy and we often lived without including, at times, without food. Despite the challenges, my parents instilled in me a strong work ethic and the belief that education was the key to a brighter future. With their unwavering support, I managed to excel academically and developed a thirst for knowledge that would propel me forward for the rest of my life.

After graduating high school by taking every honors level

class I could my senior year, I set my sights on attending college. However, financial constraints threatened to derail my dreams. With relentless dedication, I earned a scholarship and other educational funding to attend my local branch of the University of Texas, where I majored in computer science.

After completing my Bachelor of Science and Master of Science degrees, my journey truly began when I landed my first professional job at PriceWaterhouseCoopers Consulting. At PwC, I honed my expertise in technology and management, gaining invaluable experience in client engagements across various industries. I subsequently obtained a Master of Business Administration (MBA) at Webster University to diverse my deep technical background.

My career was then altered when PwC was acquired by IBM, a renowned global technology company. At IBM, I further honed my skills and expanded my professional network, immersing myself in diverse projects that spanned continents. My leadership abilities started to shine through as I successfully spearheaded high-stakes initiatives and transformed struggling divisions into profitable ventures.

Driven by a thirst for more knowledge, I embarked on a new chapter in my career, joining Dell, a trailblazer in the tech industry. The fast-paced environment pushed me to my limits as the Consulting Manager for Latin America, but I took on the challenge, leveraging my expertise to drive innovation and push the boundaries of what was possible. My contributions propelled Dell's growth and cemented my reputation as a respected industry leader.

However, my journey came full circle when I returned to IBM in my current role as the Global Managed Services Leader. With wisdom acquired from my years of experience, I spearheaded large-scale initiatives, leveraging my expertise toward continued success. My life philosophy is "If you love what you are doing, you will be successful." My unwavering passion for my work, mentoring others, and continuous resilience in the face of adversity keeps propelling me to greater heights. My remarkable journey, which has propelled me from poverty to the esteemed position as a Partner executive at IBM, serves as a powerful testament to the transformative power that lies within the pursuit of one's true passion.

BIOGRAPHY

Ricardo Diaz is the youngest son of a family of eight brothers and sisters to immigrant parents. His dad is from Spain and his mom is from Mexico. He was the first sibling to complete graduate and post-graduate university studies at the University of Texas at El Paso, majoring in computer science. He completed his MBA at Webster University to round out his deep technical skills with business fundamentals focused on enterprise financial management. He is an avid cycling fan and rides his road bike at every opportunity. Ricardo's rides usually total between sixty-five to eighty miles per week. He lives in Austin, Texas, with his spouse and three children.

¡AHORA, SÍ VEO!

IRIS V. FERNANDEZ

"I was born ignorant, but I'll die vegan!"

I wasn't always vegan. As a matter of fact, I grew up in the projects in the Bronx, eating plenty of meat and seafood because my dad was a chef and had access to the best cuts. I am not trying to convince anyone of my lifestyle, but I want to demonstrate how my vegan lifestyle was incorporated into my Puerto Rican background.

I remember having a tantrum at lunchtime in my tweens because mi mami offered to make me a hamburger (homemade from ground beef) while waiting for my pork chops with rice and beans! Back then I was very scrawny and anemic, so mi mami would accommodate my wants.

When I had my own children, I tried eating healthier for their sake. I became a nurse and took more interest in our nutrition but still ate too much meat and seafood products. I then vowed never to give up pork or all my cheeses!!

At 62, my adult daughter asked me to watch *What the Health* with her. This documentary discusses (among other issues) how the American diet is high in animal products contributing to the standard American diseases, diabetes, heart disease, and cancer. The very next day my daughter and I cleared out all our fridge and cupboards of anything that was not plant-based and there was a lot. We both denounced our previous lifestyle and it happened to fall on the day of mi mami's anniversary of her passing. We now celebrate that day in memory of her. We both wished we could have been enlightened while she was still alive and maybe mi mami might have lived longer and healthier than her ninety years.

The more I researched about the vegan lifestyle, the more I realized that it was not just about our health but the health of the animals and our planet. What I had always craved was not the dead animal but the seasonings. I learned to season vegetables and fruits to satisfy my cravings and I have learned to "veganize" many of my favorite childhood dishes, including Puerto Rican roast pork, pernil, with marinated jackfruit. I can even make bacalaitos without any codfish by using canned hearts of palm and adding seaweed sheets to the batter to get that umami flavoring.

I go to bed each night knowing I did not contribute to any beings' suffering and that makes my soul shine! By the way, as for vegans not getting enough vitamin B12, both my daughter and I had to cut down on our B12 supplements because we were on the higher recommended levels in our lab work. I now have been fully vegan for five-and-a-half years and not only am I at my healthiest, my vision has improved each year. I'm due for a new set of eyeglasses which will not be progressives but just for reading.

I was born ignorant, but I'll die vegan!

BIOGRAPHY

Iris V. Fernandez put herself through nursing school as a single mom of two young children in the 1980s. Her career varied, serving her community as a Staff Nurse, Case Manager, and Quality Assurance Manager, serving as a Diabetes Educator and a Research Nurse at New York Presbyterian Hospital. She was one of two registered nurses (RNs) working in a telemedicine project servicing the mostly Latino elderly community in Manhattan until she got her Master of Science in Nursing (MSN) from Columbia University at fifty. She was a clinical analyst who mentored nurses in nursing informatics for the last fifteen years of her career at "Magnet™" designated hospitals until 2020 when she retired. She is a founding Co-author of *Latinas 100: Leaving a Legacy and Inspiring the Next Generation* and Co-author of *Hispanic Rising Stars, Vol. III.* She now spends her time writing (a memoir), gardening, and sharing her "veganized" Puerto Rican dishes.

LUIS ENRIQUE FERNÁNDEZ TORRES

"The last thing I'll ever do is give up."

I was born and raised in La Habana, Cuba, by a single mother of two, who gave up her career as a teacher to be a full-time mother. It was the late 1990s in Cuba; the economic outlook was not great, and even though we had a big portion of our family in the United States (US), remittances and care packages were not enough to keep our family afloat.

So, my mother—the most hardworking and relentless person I know—started selling croquettes and flans and working any job that came her way. She even went as far as to co-run a horticulture sales business just to make ends meet. She faced every challenge to give my sister and me a better future.

It was with that goal in mind, that after more than twenty attempts to get a visa to move to the US, in 2010 we obtained one under a US family reunification program. We took our flight to freedom to Miami, where we had to start from nothing. Once there, my mother took jobs working in factories and retail stores, as well as cleaning offices and schools. She frequently held three jobs at a time just to put food in our mouths, so my sister and I could focus on school. While in high school, my sister and I started working at McDonald's to help pay the bills, and we were determined to make it work.

My mother's relentless spirit, work ethic, and dedication have taught me to believe in myself and my capabilities. She has taught me that with hard work and resilience, we can accomplish anything we set our minds to, no matter how hard and unforgiving the journey may be. She has always told me that hard work beats talent and the odds. This is why I always say that *the last thing I'll ever do is give up.*

It is with her same resilience that I learned English from scratch in under two years after arriving in the US. I took her determination and applied it to my academic pursuits, which led me to receive scholarships to several universities. It was her unwavering attitude that carried me through my time at the University of Florida just five years after moving to the US—and ultimately led me to become the first college graduate in my family.

Today, I am the personification of her undeniable resilience. I recently graduated with my Master's Degree from Georgetown University, becoming the first in my family to accomplish this—and this is just the beginning. Her lesson on overcoming adversity motivates me to be the best version of myself every day. When I reflect on all that I have accomplished in the past thirteen years, I am in awe, but more importantly, reminded of where it all began—

my inspiring mother. As I move forward, I will continue to work hard and never give up on our dream to have a better life with each passing day.

BIOGRAPHY

Luis Enrique Fernández Torres is a Project Consultant at APCO's Washington, DC, office supporting APCO's Ideas and UN teams, as well as new business development efforts for various industries and markets, especially Latin America and the Caribbean. He holds a Bachelor of Arts in International Studies with a concentration in Latin American and Caribbean Studies from the University of Florida and a Master of Professional Studies in Public Relations' and Corporate Communications from Georgetown University. Originally from La Habana, Cuba, Luis migrated to the United States at age twelve and has a passion for creative expression.

BECOMING THE OWNER OF A LIFE CANVAS

SUJEILY FONSECA-GONZALEZ

"You own the canvas of your life, and you can paint on it as much as you want!"

Life comes with challenges that we must learn to overcome to become the painter on our life canvas. On the path toward our goals, we must be our greatest believer. This is my story and how I learned to be the owner of my life canvas, and to empower others to be the owner of their life canvas.

I was born and raised in Puerto Rico, coming from a family of five. I decided to pursue studies in the fields of electrical and computer engineering, and practice and professional ethics. It was a challenging journey, as I had to move far from home without the support of relatives. Additionally, my family faced financial struggles, so I dedicated myself to excelling in my studies while securing scholarships and working at college and through fellowships to ease the burden of expenses. Despite facing numerous challenges, I refused to give up.

I gained valuable knowledge and skills through work and research experiences. This led me to a software engineering career path, which made me move to the United States. I worked hard to showcase my technical abilities, problem-solving skills, and dedication to diversity and inclusion. Overcoming challenges and biases became a common occurrence, as I constantly had to prove my worth and expertise, primarily because of stereotypes and prejudices due to being a woman in a male-dominated career.

At first, I was afraid of failing and what others could say. I was my greatest critic and judge. I was preventing myself from speaking and taking opportunities. I knew the solutions to problems but was afraid of raising my voice. Then, I started thinking whenever I was afraid of doing something, "What is the worst thing that could happen?" and "Who could advocate for me if I am not my greatest believer?" That helped me adopt a positive-growth mindset to embrace optimism and resiliency. My determination and mindset propelled my professional growth, leading me to my current role as a Software Engineering Manager.

As a Hispanic woman in engineering, I became a trailblazer, inspiring others to pursue their career path. I create and support initiatives for skill enhancements, equal opportunities, and a sense of community. I started to become the voice of those afraid to speak up and enable them to become the painters of their life canvas.

Believing in the power of "us" is crucial. People can learn so much from others' experiences, and we can rise when we uplift and empower others to rise with us. Our minds can work for or against us. On our way, we will find many barriers and obstacles preventing us from seeing our target as attainable. It is up to us to decide whether to stop before these difficulties or to move forward even stronger. Don't fear fighting for your dreams or let negativity invade your thoughts. You own the canvas of your life, and you can paint on it as much as you want!

BIOGRAPHY

Sujeily Fonseca-Gonzalez is a Puerto Rican with studies in electrical and computer engineering, and practice and professional ethics. She conducted research in video games, education, machine learning, embedded systems, etc., of which she authored or co-authored research papers. Sujeily had multiple leadership and development roles. She is a Software Engineering Manager for IBM MultiCloud SaaS Platform, leading high-performing teams, collaborating with stakeholders and clients, and driving Agile ceremonies and social and growth activities. Sujeily leads Employee Resource Group (ERG) and Business Resource Group (BRG) initiatives through the IBM Hispanic Executive Council and drives technical symposiums and initiatives through the IBM Carolinas Technical Expert Council. She has achieved corporate awards and is a Career Mentor and Coach.

JANET GOMEZ

*"Nothing good comes easy. Keep pushing forward, keep striving
for that dream, and I promise the good will come your way."*

I turned thirty-three in March 2023. When I reflect on how
much change has happened these past three-and-a-half years,
A LOT has happened. I got laid off from a job I had for almost
eight years. I had my second child. We lived through a pandemic.
My youngest was hospitalized. I got a fantastic opportunity as a
Marketing Assistant at a shopping center, and within a year, I quit
corporate life to work full-time on my business. I had some bad
moments, but so much good also has happened.

I was on the journey of working on my business full time
for more than seven years. I had a deep yearning for what I so
desperately wanted. I worked as a Fashion Jewelry Designer and
Merchandiser for almost eight years; the last four years were the
worst. I had a boss who made me feel incompetent. She would
chuckle when I would show her a project I had worked on so

hard, implying it was terrible. I remember I would hate driving to downtown Los Angeles. I would hate leaving my girls behind. I would hate having to drive up the parking lot. I would stay in my car for ten minutes and feel the air get sucked out of me. I felt a pit in my stomach, and I would cry. This was EVERY DAY. My spirit was dying, and I wasn't myself anymore.

It was the worst feeling; I don't wish that on anyone. My boss and the higher-ups frequently belittled me, and when I tried to express my feelings, I was never heard. I never saw the light at the end of the tunnel.

I am sharing this because you are not alone if YOU feel this way in your current job. I was around so much toxicity and people constantly making me feel less than others.

The path you are currently on will take you to the one that God has already created for you. Nothing good comes easy. Keep pushing forward, keep striving for that dream, and I promise the good will come your way. I now work full time for my creative consulting studio, where I help small businesses bring their best post forward on social media, among other creative services.

BIOGRAPHY

Janet Gomez is a mother of two and the founder of a creative consulting studio, Jan's Spring Design, and holds a degree in Fashion Merchandising. She specializes in social media management and conceptualizes and designs the perfect layouts for brands! Her experience as a fashion merchandiser and in marketing has allowed her to partner with brands such as Target, PopSugar, and Aerie and helped her grow her business with more than twelve clients.

CHASING DR. GÓMEZ

JESSICA GÓMEZ

"Unsure how my story could make a difference, I soon realized that my platform can raise awareness on the dental disparities that my Hispanic people face."

My mother embraced me as I shut the door to my dorm for the last time. She tearily whispered, "I never thought we'd have a daughter like you."

"A daughter like me?" I thought. I only ever called home to complain about how hard adjusting to college was. I rarely visited as I spent every minute studying or working. I slowly became a stranger to my family.

Providing a better life for their children led my grandparents to immigrate from México to inner-city Chicago. As my parents began to navigate life on their own, they were quickly enveloped by the dangers that surrounded them. My father, a victim of police brutality, married my mother, who survived on government assistance. Although neither of them saw an opportunity to attend college, they instilled the importance of education in all four of their children.

As a Latina in dentistry, I'm constantly reminded of the oral health disparities my people face. For example, we future providers struggle with lack of representation in the field. I can see why, as becoming a dentist seems nearly impossible without mentors or financial resources. During my time as a dental assistant, I learned of the many health disparities faced by Latinx patients. The consequences of said disparities are no match for the inadequate oral health education and resources these communities receive. Language barriers, cultural differences, and financial obstacles prevent patients from accessing the care they deserve.

In December 2022, my piece "La Pequeña Dentista Que Sí Pudo" was published in the fourth volume of the *Today's Inspired Young Latina* book series. Within those pages, I speak on my struggles as a first-generation college student who aspired to become a public health dentist. My chapter was also the first time I publicly spoke about my eating disorder.

My publication reached Latinx-Milwaukee communities slowly but surely. I soon found myself speaking to crowds of Latinx students about the importance of following their dreams. And there I was, featured on the front page of a newspaper, pictured right next to Latina legend, Celia Cruz! Although I loved connecting with Latinx-Milwaukee this way, imposter syndrome crept in. Unsure how my story could make a difference, I soon realized that my platform can raise awareness on the dental disparities that my Hispanic people face.

A month later, I launched the first behavioral dentistry research lab at the Marquette University School of Dentistry. Our research focuses on the biopsychosocial differences in dental patients with an eating disorder. I hope our findings better educate others on the relationships between dentistry and eating disorders—resulting in patients receiving exceptional care. I'm thankful for the period in my life when I struggled with bulimia, as it has enabled me to provide better care to my future patients.

I envision myself as a dentist who goes above and beyond for her patients. I dream of impacting others through accessible education and groundbreaking research. I empathize with the struggles faced by minority, low-income, and underserved patients. At twenty-three years old, there's plenty I'm uncertain about. Yet, I couldn't be more certain about my vocation as a dentist that strives to better our world one tooth at a time.

BIOGRAPHY

Jessica Gómez is the oldest of four Mexican-American children. She grew up in Oak Lawn, Illinois, and attended Marquette University for her Honors Bachelor's Degree in Psychology and Biological Sciences. Jessica will be spending the next four years at the University of Iowa, studying to obtain her Doctor of Dental Surgery (DDS) degree. Aside from writing, Jessica has a passion for advocating for and guiding other first-generation college students. She is a committed researcher, presenting her work at national conferences. She aims to one day open many doors for Latina women who aspire to go into dentistry by creating a scholarship fund.

WHAT WE PRIORITIZE GETS OUR ATTENTION

DEBBIE GONZALEZ

"Life is fragile and we get to choose how to savor it."

From early on, I learned to put work before joy. Saturday mornings were reserved for cleaning. Nothing else could happen until the chores were done. While Mami did the heavy lifting when it came to los haceres de la casa, she imprinted on me the value of a job well-done as a top priority. My sisters and I laugh about it, but that message played a significant role in my career.

In our society, prioritizing work is synonymous with a good work ethic. I certainly received praise for my commitment to working hard. The more praise received, which often came with more tasks, the more I put work first. Slowly, my habits increasingly led to unreasonable demands of my energy and emotions.

It started out simply like staying late to provide extra activities for the students. Then, as my colleague volunteered for extra administrative duties, I stayed late to help her. How could helping a colleague be a bad thing? Besides, I learned from Mami to go above and beyond and expect nothing in return. How many hours did she spend using her talents to support her school? A job well done required sacrifice. Right?

As my career progressed and I stepped into larger roles, I normalized doing too much regardless of the company or my role. Heck, I judged anyone who didn't show the same unrelenting work ethic. I wore as a badge of honor routinely getting in early and staying late. Casual praise from a higher up reinforced the behavior. I doubled down at a cost to my emotional wellness. I didn't see how much I changed.

In fairness, it happened over many jobs. Dancing brings me joy, but I stopped attending dance classes because I could not predict when my work day ended. I love my family and celebrating milestones, but I missed my niece's grade school graduation because as I prepared to leave the office, I asked a colleague if she needed help. Many a night I pushed staying later until I literally ran to the garage to get my car before they closed. Over time, I justified choosing work versus what brought me joy—I made a difference and people depended on me. But I cried too many times, feeling overwhelmed. Even a dinner date with hubby seemed difficult to plan. Bitterness began to set into me. When my job ended, I reinvented myself. Los cantasos enseñan.

Sitting across from Mami one morning, I pondered why God had given me this time. I told her I broke old behavior patterns and planned to enjoy it. Two years later, Mami died. I am forever grateful that my job ended, which afforded me the ability to have more fun and created precious memories. As a coach, I emphasize striving for balance and paying attention to the happy moments. Life is fragile and we get to choose how to savor it. It helps to be reminded that our narratives can be rewritten to align with what we hold dear.

BIOGRAPHY

Debbie Gonzalez, shares emotional intelligence (EQ) strategies for high-achieving Black, Indigenous, People of Color (BIPOC) women in leadership roles to navigate towards striving for balance and allowing more joy in their lives. High-achieving BIPOC women tend to push themselves beyond the level of burnout. Debbie is a first-generation Latina Social Worker, and certified professional coach. With Debbie's unique style of leadership coaching and interactive learning experiences, leaders grant themselves the psychological permission to change habits that no longer serve them, improving their effectiveness and overall wellbeing. Debbie found joy in publishing her children's picture books.

THE FIRE

LEOPOLDO GOUT

"Our most valuable connections aren't made through adherence to the norms but finding those who stray from them the same way we do."

I grew up in Mexico City with little money but a wealth of ideas, books, and artists. Seemingly every day my mother, Andrea Valeria, was entertaining more incredible writers, adventurers, poets, musicians, and scientists in our house, staying up into the early hours talking and drinking and smoking. As a kid, I'd listen as long as I could stay awake, excited and enamored by the ribaldry.

By the time I finished high school, I had earned a full scholarship to study sculpture at London's famed Central Saint Martins School of Art. After receiving my education, I wandered the globe a bit, living wild days out of a suitcase for a few years and landing my first solo show in Manhattan at Tricia Collins Contemporary Art. New York opened up for me, revealing its endless winding paths. I squatted my first studio with the generous

Ray Smith and the equally talented and mercurial Saint Clair Cemin, hosting other artists, including Ron Gorchov to Vik Muniz, who would wander in from the wilds.

From a very young age, I would make art that was part drawing and part performance, adding theatricality to my drawings of battles in the oceans and stars by literally setting them on fire. I did set the couch on fire making one of these drawings-come-to-life, an incident that seemingly foreshadowed the loss of home and much of my artwork in a blaze in New York later in life. Though it was also this added story and life to art which similarly foreshadowed my entry into cinema.

After my first show, I met the late extraordinary dealer Jack Tilton who encouraged me to do another show, which turned into a bizarre performance drawing with a contortionist and an afterparty which got so out of hand I receive messages about it to this day. Days later I went to see Jack, worried he thought I was a total basket case, but he said, "Leopoldo, we sold the piece. Stay weird and let me worry about how to work with that." It sparked a fire I carry in me to this day. It wasn't normality which had drawn me and Jack together; our most valuable connections aren't made through adherence to the norms but finding those who stray from them the same way we do.

I still have an active studio practice with commissions and acquisitions to collectors and spaces all over the world. But I also make successful films, television, documentaries, books, and even video games based on my graphic novels. All this, though, is only possible with that inner fire, the desire to bring to life ideas, to push my weirdness out into the world. I try to emulate and echo that fleeting moment when you wake up from a vivid dream, where you smelled and felt things as real that very quickly dissipate and disappear into the fog only seconds after you wake up. My work lives in between that disappearing space, like drawings simultaneously coming to life and being consumed in fire.

BIOGRAPHY

Besides having work in galleries around the world, Leopoldo Gout has written, published, and produced films, documentaries, television, and books for more than a decade. He and co-author, Ana Aridjis, are turning their book, *Monarca*, into an experiential installation taking the audience on the journey of the Monarch butterflies from Canada to Mexico. He co-wrote Netflix's *The Chosen One* with Everardo Gout based on Mark Millar's American Jesus. His fifth and most recent novel, *Piñata*, is being adapted by a major studio; and Leopoldo produced the enthralling docuseries, Carlos, about fellow immigrant Carlos Santana's Latin-gone-psychedelic rock 'n' roll life.

A JOURNEY OF DETERMINATION, FOOD EXPLORATION, AND STRONGER FAMILY BONDS

ALEJANDRA GRAF

"Embrace the uncertainty of the future, secure in the knowledge that you will flourish wherever you might be."

In the hopeful year of 2010, my husband and I packed our car, securely buckled in our kids, and off we went, filled with optimism to create a new life. Our journey took us from Monterrey, Mexico, to Austin, Texas. Why, you may ask? Our goal was to create a future full of opportunities and fairness, free from societal judgments or ingrained norms for our kids. We imagined an environment where our children and ourselves could pursue our passions and thrive.

We had no plan, nor were our paths guaranteed. We had no savings, no beaming credit score, and no jobs. But we were determined to navigate this new world. The only thing clear was that we were going to make it.

From the moment we set foot in our new city, we decided

to be receptive and open. We committed ourselves to embrace diversity—in cultures, people, and even food—and to grasp every unique experience that came our way. Reflecting, the journey was a challenging one. Yet, every obstacle was solvable; and every hardship became a lesson. Arriving in Austin, a city poised on food culture, particularly in vegan cuisine, felt serendipitous. Gradually, I honed my culinary skills, exploring new flavors and finding my rhythm in the kitchen. My dishes, or culinary experiments as my kids called them, evolved from "What is this?" to an enthusiastic "Wow!" around the dinner table.

With each dish, I discovered the power of food to uplift spirits, to foster connections, and to build friendships. I realized that my purpose in life is closely tied to the power of food, sharing my recipes and inspiring people to add more vegetables and home-cooked meals to their diets.

Two years later, we moved to Houston, but now it was different. Our path was more apparent; well, at least we knew it would be okay. It also marked the time when I was ready to start working. I enrolled in an Art History Master's Program, asking for a refund a couple of weeks after reading a quote from Danielle LaPorte's *Fire Starter Sessions* book: "What do people thank you for?" I knew what lit me up and people thanked me for are my recipes and ability to cook.

Moving to a different country was a challenging experience that made me realize I had more strength than I thought. I learned how to build a diverse and lively community and gained the ability to motivate others to enjoy cooking and sharing meals through a now thriving business, my blogs, "Piloncillo&Vainilla" and "AleCooks."

I also rediscovered how we Latins love the importance of family bonding over meals, regrouping at least once a day, and the joy of sharing about our lives around the dinner table. The experience facilitated heartwarming conversations that strengthened our family bonds.

We discovered that our family is an unstoppable force by being open-minded and open-hearted. When we work together and support one another, there is no obstacle we cannot conquer. Our journey taught us to respect and to love our dual heritage—Mexico as the cradle of our past and the United States as the vibrant canvas of our present.

BIOGRAPHY

Alejandra Graf is a Mexican food lover and wellness pusher that follows a plant-based diet. She has a degree in Art History and a Professional Certification as a Plant-based Cook. A few years ago, she became the voice behind "Piloncillo&Vainilla" and "AleCooks," bilingual blogs about her experiences, food philosophy, and recipes. Alejandra lives in Houston, Texas, with her husband and three kids.

IF YOU PERSEVERE, YOU WILL ACHIEVE YOUR DREAMS

SARA GUTIERREZ

"Never give up on your dreams because while they may not come easy, they can be achieved with patience and perseverance."

I was born in a small town in the northwest area of Mexico, where my parents gave me more than I could ever imagine. They were loving and wise. They gave me security, and they provided a fruitful education. Their wisdom had a lasting impact on my life. My mother would always say, "Sarita, El que persevera alcanza," which means, if you have a dream, especially if it's challenging, you can achieve them if you are determined and continue to fight for them.

Since I was a child, I always knew that I wanted to become a biologist. I have always loved animals and the natural world really intrigued me. So, after I finished high school, I applied to the Universidad Nacional de Mexico (UNAM) to study biology and was fortunately admitted. Moving away from my family and friends to college in a big city was difficult, especially because topics, such as math and physics were not easy subjects for me. My father could sense that I was struggling and recommended that I come home. It was tempting, but I decided against it after reflecting on my mom's saying, "El que persevera alcanza." Four years later, I finished my degree while pursuing a thesis in the Atmospheric Sciences Department and I continued a master program in ecology.

It was during my two-year Master Program at UNAM, where I met my future husband. He was applying to PhD programs in Physics at the University of New Mexico; and so naturally I wanted to extend my education in the United States as well. I applied for a graduate program in medical sciences and was able to secure a scholarship for the program. The program ended up being much more difficult than I anticipated, which was exacerbated by my poor understanding of the English language. After many days and weeks of sleeplessness and frustration, my mother's words of wisdom would repeat in my head to keep me going "El que persevera alcanza". Sure enough, three years later I presented my defense and was awarded my degree.

Our family started growing during this time and because my husband was offered a job in Boston, we moved to the Northeast, where the Biotech Industry was booming. I applied to MilliporeSigma, a business of Merck KGaA, where I was able to fulfill my dream of working as a scientist on the Research and Development Group. At Millipore I learned a lot. I had the opportunity to travel, presenting our work at trade conferences, publishing some papers, and contributing to patents for products that madetheir way to the market.

Now that I am retired, I can reflect on the two biggest lessons I've learned in my life. The first is to never give up on your dreams because while they may not come easy; they can be achieved with patience and perseverance. The second is that we must all become lifelong learners. Knowledge is power.

BIOGRAPHY

Sara Gutierrez was born in Tepic Nay, Mexico. She earned a Bachelor of Science degree in Biology and a Master of Science degree in Ecology from UNAM in Mexico City. She moved to United states at the age of twenty-five, where she got Master degree in Medical Sciences in Albuquerque, New Mexico. After graduation, she moved to Massachusetts, where she worked as a Scientist in Research and Development. She was the team lead in various projects, collaborated in the development of cutting-edge products, and is co-author in several scientific papers. She is retired after twenty-five years of service at MilliporeSigma. Sara lives in Seattle, Washington.

EVERY OVERNIGHT SENSATION WAS TEN YEARS IN THE MAKING

ELISA HERNANDEZ

"No more working in silence."

I'm a first-generation Salvadoran, Latina woman working in sports. At the start of my career, I always thought it was better to work in silence. Work hard, keep your head down, and someday your hard work would pay off. I thought overly showcasing your work and accomplishments would come off the wrong way. I was wrong. No more working in silence. If you don't believe in yourself no one will, and you will find yourself on the outside of rooms where decisions are made that will determine your future. You need to speak up and, trust me, you will never regret that you did.

Working in a male dominated field, you have to find your voice. I noticed colleagues were getting promotions and, yet, I was struggling to move up. Instead of speaking up, I told myself I must not have done enough; and I will continue to work hard, and they soon will see my value. They didn't, until I spoke up and told them my value. I have worked at companies where, at times, I was the only Latina in the room, and the only person that spoke Spanish. This began to open my eyes to how much representation matters and it was up to me to speak up.

I ran the NFL's only US Latino bicultural account for two years. The platform started out as an assignment and turned into much more. A simple Instagram account became a platform for Latino players, Spanish announcers, Latino NFL reporters and fans. As a content strategist and digital host of the channel, I realized my decisions determined how we would highlight Latinos in the NFL. They say football es familia. Football es cultura. During my time there we created "Pass the Mic" and in collaboration with the NFL's main account would highlight the best Spanish call of the week. I did features on the NFL's top Spanish announcers, like Adrian Garcia-Marquez who is Mexican; Moises Linares, who is Salvadoran; and Carlos Bohorquez, who is from Venezuela. There's beauty in seeing yourself in a sport you love so much, to give inspiration to young professionals that you belong in America's game.

The highest form of my "No more working in silence" came in 2023. Along with the talented cleat designer SolesBySir, who is Cuban, I launched a cleat initiative during Latino Heritage month. I partnered with five NFL clubs and four NFL players to showcase their Latino pride and teach their position names in Spanish. Taking a chance showcased Latino culture from Pittsburgh, Pennsylvania, with Najee Harris to London, England, with Chris Olave.

The work isn't over, and despite me moving on from the NFL, I realized the importance of telling these stories no matter where I go. No working in silence no matter where I land and continuing to be who I am and represent where I come from. Things take time, trust yourself and understand you will get to where you need to be. Use your voice.

BIOGRAPHY

Elisa Hernandez is a Salvadoran bilingual host, producer, editor and two-time Emmy winner working in the Los Angeles area. Elisa became the Los Angeles Dodgers Stadium host in 2022. She hosts the Dodgers LIVE 30-minute pregame show, as well as in-game segments. She recently hosted the 2022 MLB Celebrity All-Star game doing field interviews, in-game segments, and introducing musical talent. She was at the NFL for six years and was the digital host of ElSnapNFL, which was the NFL's only US Latino-focused Instagram account from 2021 to 2023. In 2021, she also launched her own podcast, Sports-Ish, on the Bleav Podcast Network.

MAYHEM ACCENTUATED BY
BYSTANDERS

MONICA ISIS IBARRA

". . . a reminder of knowing my value, and to not expend my energy on those who do not see or acknowledge me."

The past is not blurry in this story of being bullied. With the clarify of time and knowledge, bystanders can play distinct roles in bullying situations.

Let me share with you how I got here. The setting is a school cafeteria in the early eighties, nothing fancy. Just a plain-Jane run-of-the-mill lunchroom with what I recall being yellowish subway tiles on the walls. Row upon row of tables. As usual, I am sitting with my bestie Karry; she is to my right.

On this day, I hear shouting that is leaving me unsettled. It is a voice from a boy calling my name. It is so odd because I typically do not have people, let alone boys, calling my name. My Spidey senses are tingling as I have a healthy mistrust of boys, all males in fact. As an immigrant Latina living in rural America, I had a healthy distrust of everyone, which was a safe tactic to navigate spaces. This white kid, let's call him Bob, keeps shouting. Over and over. A little louder each time. Now I am getting pissed—not frustrated—pissed! This kid was calling attention to me and the tactic of "ignoring" and silence are not working as an effective method to be left alone. The shouting goes on for what felt like hours; it was in actuality, just a few minutes. How long is a lunch period in middle school, right? Karry leans closer to inquire how I can keep ignoring this fool calling my name above the crowded lunchroom. As a last-ditch effort, Bob shouts. "Hey Jungle Bunny!" Huh? I think. I am Mexican and that slur he chose to call me is not meant for Latinos. I am sure I smiled and choose to not respond as I already am aware this would not be a quick response. I choose to continue with my silence and move on.

The lesson on that day? Bullies usually have a sense of entitlement and superiority over others, and lack compassion, impulse control, and social skills. On that day, three of the four types of bystanders, folks who are present at an event or incident but do not take part, were in the room. The outsiders sat quietly, along with me, saying nothing and not getting involved. In this case, it was not only the students, but it was also the adults in the room, the teachers and the staff. All of them, standing and silently enabling and permitting Bob to openly bully me. *The reinforcers* were in full fledge mode here with actively supporting Bob in his behavior through laughter and cheers. Then there was Karry, the sole *defender* in the room. Who quietly wished and implored me to take active action versus the passivity I had chosen to successfully implement.

The lesson, a reminder of knowing my value and to not expend my energy on those who do not see or acknowledge me. On this day, silence was my friend and I lived to fight another day.

BIOGRAPHY

As an equity, inclusion, and diversity (EID/DEI) practitioner, Monica Isis Ibarra has focused her efforts on aligning with inclusion, aligning policies with intent versus. impact to provide access, and opportunities as strategies and tactics to drive equitable practices impacting people. Monica was the 2021 ACLU of Minnesota (ACLU-Mn) Volunteer of the Year award winner and a delegate for the 2022 United Nations Latino Leadership Summit. She was pointed to the Health Equity Advisory and Leadership (HEAL) Council in 2022, which assists the Minnesota Department of Human Service in developing strong performance measures for advancing health equity.

CLARA LUCIA JARAMILLO-CARRIER

"It was always about what other people needed and how I could help others, but there was no talk about the importance of self-care and pursuing your dreams."

When I was four years old, I was interviewed by the psychologist of a bilingual school my mom wanted me to attend. She asked me to draw something. So, I drew a picture of my mom, dad, and little sister. When she looked at it, she asked me, "How come none of these people in the picture have arms?"

I told her it was because my dad never hugged me.

From that moment on, I associated my inability to be loved, affirmed, embraced, and accepted as my fault. There had to be something wrong with me for my dad to not hug me.

As a result, I realized that I had to strive to be a good girl. I had to work hard to deserve to be loved, and that became my focus. I became an A student and was someone people would look to for support. I was the responsible child.

I developed beliefs around how I'd better be the perfect child. I'd better obey and follow the rules so that one day I would be deserving of the love and affection, not only of my dad but of everyone else in the world. I associated love and affirmation with how much I could do and how much perfectionism I could achieve.

The other piece that goes with that is—we grew up as Catholics. There was this hovering notion of giving. It was always about what other people needed and how I could help others, but there was no talk about the importance of self-care and pursuing your dreams.

It wasn't until I enrolled in a self-learning and developmental program about social-emotional intelligence that I began to discover another way of living and being. I learned that underneath my desire to help, I was creating codependency.

This realization was eye-opening. I was spending all of this time, effort, energy, and resources doing things for people instead of being with them, empowering them, and providing the tools for them to do it themselves. I was fishing for them, instead of teaching them how to fish for themselves.

Six months later, I entered a master's program for transformational leadership and coaching. I learned that self-care is not something that we should only be given by our parents when we are little; but it's something that we can pursue now as adults.

I can become my own mother. I can be sweet to myself. I can ask myself, "How are you feeling?" I can be kind and patient. I don't have to be doing, striving, and serving all the time. I can pause and practice, little by little, to love, appreciate, and affirm myself. And when I want those things from other people, I can simply ask for them.

Today, I teach others how to practice this way of being. In the process, it's my goal that they would feel seen, heard, and appreciated and have a different and more loving perception of themselves. Seeing that fills me with pure joy!

BIOGRAPHY

Clara Lucia Jaramillo-Carrier is an expert in transformational leadership and coaching with more than 40,000 hours of studying and training to her credit. A proud Colombian American, she is a speaker and founder of Awaken Your Purpose and Breaking Through Consulting & Coaching. With more than twenty years in the corporate world as a strategist, communicator, marketer, and journalist, Clara Lucia holds a Master of Arts in Transformational Leadership and Coaching and two graduate certificates from Wright Graduate University, one in emotional intelligence and another in transformational coaching. She is also an Associated Certified Coach through the International Coaching Federation.

FROM CURIOSITY TO CALLING: HOW A CACAO CEREMONY RECONNECTED ME TO MY HERITAGE

EMILY JIMENEZ

"In discovering the roots of my family's past, I found the strength to shape a future grounded in my heritage."

I walked into the apartment alone, wide eyed and super curious. Just the night before I saw a post advertising a Dominican Mother's Day themed cacao ceremony; and despite not exactly knowing what cacao was, I just knew I had to attend. Little did I know that this event would facilitate a profound connection to my ancestry and bring me closer to my family.

Seated on the floor in a circle with mujeres I didn't know, I took a deep breath and trusted that I was in the right place. The hosts welcomed us in, guided us on setting an intention for our time together, and served everyone a cup of ceremonial cacao—a hot chocolate beverage made from heirloom strains of cacao from Central and South America.

As the ceremony unfolded, I felt a sense of belonging that I had never experienced before. Listening to their relatable stories of the roles Latinas play in our families made me feel seen and comfortable to share about my personal experience as a first-generation daughter of Dominican immigrants living in New York City.

At the end of the ceremony, I knew I had to share this experience with my family and friends. I asked the facilitator about her availability to host a ceremony for my birthday that was coming up in a few weeks; but she shared that she was going on sabbatical for a year overseas and would be unavailable during that time.

Disappointed but undeterred, I began searching for other facilitators in my area, hoping to find someone who could guide me through this sacred experience. Surprisingly, no suitable facilitators were available nearby. The call to share the magic of cacao with others grew louder within me and I made the decision to become one.

Guided by an inner compass, I sought out training that led me on a pilgrimage to Guatemala, where I learned more about cacao from Mayan elders. I absorbed their wisdom like a sponge and allowed their decolonized teachings to shape and mold me.

As I delved deeper into my studies, I discovered an ancestral connection to cacao. Conversations with family members revealed that my maternal grandfather had cultivated cacao in the countryside of the Dominican Republic. Each tale they shared weaved a stronger bond among us, bridging the gap between generations and deepening my appreciation for our shared heritage. This ignited a newfound sense of purpose in me. I felt a responsibility to honor the legacy of my family and the indigenous cultures that had revered cacao for centuries.

Equipped with this newfound knowledge, I began incorporating indigenous teachings and practices into my work at universities and corporate spaces. In discovering the roots of my family's past, I found the strength to shape a future grounded in my heritage. Today, I stand as a proud facilitator, a bridge between the past and the present, the old and the new.

The cacao ceremony not only introduced me to the rich history and significance of Cacao but also served as a catalyst for my personal and professional growth. I learned that by honoring our roots and embracing our cultural heritage, we can find a sense of belonging and purpose.

BIOGRAPHY

Emily Jimenez is the eldest child of Dominican immigrants, the first to attend college, obtain a graduate degree and work in a corporate setting. She has twenty years' experience in the non-profit sector supporting women and young adults. This experience has fueled her passion for being a fierce advocate of equity in education, finding culturally competent mentors and workplace wellness. In 2020 she launched TheManifestationMami.com, a virtual wellness space where she guides busy professionals on how to trust their intuition and make strategic moves in service of their purpose and career through a unique blend of spirituality and career development.

HOW I OVERCAME ADVERSITY AS LGBTQ+ LEADER BREAKING BOUNDARIES IN PROFESSIONAL SPORTS

ELIUD JIMENEZ

"Work hard, then dream big."

Born and raised in Hale Center, Texas, I quickly discovered my love for sports. But as one of twelve siblings in a non-denominational Latino family, my life seemed forced down a different path. I started working in the "campo" at just the age of five, picking cotton and vegetables during summer breaks to help maintain the family household. I quickly felt the overbearing weight of trying to survive as a low-income immigrant family, and often saw my dream of working in sports as a growing impossibility. When I eventually entered high school, I only felt more marginalized when I came out as a gay Latino in rural, conservative Texas.

I knew becoming a professional athlete would be the hardest path into professional sports, so I aimed to work for a professional sports team instead. Whether it was soccer, basketball, or track and field, I always found myself drawn to the thrill of competition, the camaraderie of teammates, and the dedication required to excel in their chosen field. I quickly realized that a college education would be my gateway into the field. After high school, I enrolled at Dallas Baptist University and received my bachelor's degree and later enrolled at Keller Graduate School where I received a Master's Degree in human resources. As years went by, I wanted to compliment my degrees to set myself apart and received two paralegal specializations, which were immigration law, employment law. Then, I earned a certificate as a legal interpreter from The University of Texas at Austin (UT Austin) and worked multiple jobs—day and night—just to put myself through. In time, I lived by the mantra, "Work hard, then dream big," and secured post-grad jobs as Director of Human Resources. In 2021, my pathway to professional sports opened when I got a call from a headhunter, who asked if I was interested in interviewing to be the Director of Human Resources for FC Dallas, LLC, an MLS Sports Team.

Concerned that I would not be chosen because of my LGBTQ+ identity, to my surprise, I decided to go for the opportunity anyway, recognizing it as my one chance to break into the industry for not just myself, but other gay Latino and immigrants like me. I was stunned when I got the position, and I have set out to turn my role into one, where I not only lead human resources operations, but inspire and trailblaze a path for others who are minorities like me.

With a passion for both sports and LGBTQ+ advocacy, I have

become a driving force in breaking down barriers and promoting inclusivity within the traditionally heteronormative world of athletics. Doing so has come with its fair share of challenges. Being openly gay has caused me to face resistance and prejudice, yet rather than succumbing to societal expectations, I have chosen to embrace my true self, find strength in my authenticity, and show others that facing challenges and taking risks creates new opportunities to challenge norms, promote acceptance, and build a more inclusive future.

By fearlessly sharing my story, I hope to inspire others to never lose faith and work tirelessly to pursue their dreams, regardless of race, sexual orientation, or socio-economic status. Such qualities should never limit one's potential or hinder one's dreams, just as the young Eliud Jimenez working in the "campo" feared it might.

BIOGRAPHY

Eliud Jimenez is the Director of Human Resources for FC Dallas, LLC, an MLS Sports Team. A seasoned global human resources business partner and global talent acquisition manager, he brings over twenty years of experience advising companies on human resource matters and recruiting within the United States and other countries. He has worked in professional sports, 3PL, pharmaceuticals, insurance, oil and gas, and non-profit industries. He holds his Bachelor's and Master's degrees, and paralegal specializations, which are immigration law, employment law, from UT Austin and a Legal Interpreter Certification, also from UT Austin.

I BELIEVE YO PUEDO

DAISY ZULY KAPAHI

"It is essential to have the Jasmine Camacho-Quinn ability to jump over hurdles to reach your entrepreneur goals. You can achieve your career goals if you keep running towards them."

"I Believe Yo Puedo." Never shiftless, always hustling. Nine-to-five jobs don't exist anymore. It's all about finishing proposals at midnight and virtual meetings at 6 a.m. It is essential to have the Jasmine Camacho-Quinn ability to jump over hurdles to reach your entrepreneur goals. You can achieve your career goals if you keep running towards them. My love for my children is the track I run on. NYN EVENTS stands for Nia y Naden. My children are my motivation to work. They keep me driven and inspired with the mentality. "I Believe Yo Puedo." I started my career at ABC Television Network (ABC). I began at an entry level position and worked myself to a corner office overlooking Lincoln Center, where I produced event experiences.

There is a saying, "Moving up the ladder." I call it, "Going up the elevator" to success. Every day I went up the elevator at ABC, I promised myself that after the six-month waiting period, I was going to get a promotion. One day I walked into the elevator and saw the number twelve. I pressed the button and it was to the Human Resources Department floor. I said to myself "I Believe Yo Puedo." You guessed it, after six months I got a promotion. I pressed the elevator and got off on the twelfth floor. No fear, just determination to succeed and always make a difference.

NYN EVENTS was created with the philosophy "I Believe Yo Puedo." Clients have an idea and I bring it to life. Producing events in the city that never sleeps is extremely challenging and invigorating. Just remember these four words, "I Believe Yo Puedo." Yes, challenging and invigorating that's what I call producing fundraising events. Many events have been produced at the big apple's landmark venues Lincoln Center, The Plaza and The Pierre hotel. At these venues, I worked with clients on events, such as promotions, fundraisers, auctions and galas. New York isn't the only location I have produced events. Every location has different needs for their event lifestyles. New York is the perfect place for event consulting. I created Lunch and Learns programs addressing diabetes, stress management, back to work services and programs for mothers nursing their children. I collaborated with non-profit organizations, such as La Leche League, to provide mothers the best tools to equip them for the back-to-work transition. In Los Angeles and Washington, DC, I created yoga, ergonomics, cardiopulmonary resuscitation (CPR) and automated external defibrillator (AED) classes. Annual health fairs were produced to provide flu vaccine, mammogram and prostate screenings. These programs not only provided them healthy lifestyles but, most importantly, saved lives. An event can impact, improve and change lives. I am a proud Latina born and raised in New York City.

"The city that never sleeps." Hey, who needs to sleep when there are events to execute. NYN EVENTS continues to produce events that raise awareness, raise the bar and raise funds for communities to make a difference. I produced Asphalt Green's 50th Anniversary Gala at The Plaza hotel. Asphalt Green raised $1.2 million this year. Producing events is what I do. I leave you with these four words:

"I Believe Yo Puedo."

BIOGRAPHY

Daisy Zuly Kapahi, the founder of NYN EVENTS, was born and raised in New York City and is of Puerto Rican heritage. Her husband, Divesh Kapahi is from New Delhi, India, and they have two beautiful children, daughter Niya and son Naden. It is the multicultural household and the ever-growing diversity of New York City, which provides a platform full of ideas, consultancy and unlimited collaborations for Daisy to foster. Though her passions are creativity and innovation, it's the execution and deliverance of those ideas to life that makes the client experience especially unique. Diversity is an essential ingredient in living a flavorful authentic lifestyle. Daisy and Divesh enjoy watching their children live a NYN EVENT-ful life.

A GENERATION OF MANY FIRSTS: A JOURNEY OF PERSEVERANCE

MONIQUE LE

"Never compromise your authentic self, keep pushing through the odds while always remembering to inspire and lift others up along the way."

Growing up, I faced numerous challenges as I lived with my single mother and sister, struggling to make ends meet. We were not financially well off and it felt like the odds were stacked against me, but that never stopped me from dreaming big. As a first-generation American I experienced countless firsts in my life. HI, my name is Monique, and this is my story.

At an early age, I learned the importance of becoming independent. I took on various jobs to provide for myself and my family, refusing to let our circumstances define our future. I knew that if I wanted to create a better life for myself, I had to go beyond my boundaries.

One of my biggest goals was to pursue higher education, because that was the key to unlocking a world of opportunities.

So, I worked tirelessly, juggling multiple jobs and late-night study sessions. It was not an easy journey, but my perseverance paid off as I graduated from college with honors, becoming the first in my family to earn a degree.

But my journey didn't stop there. My passion for achieving financial independence led me to enter the financial services industry. However, the challenge of achieving many firsts is that there aren't many to lean on for advice or guidance. Instead, I looked to strangers and my curiosity led me to better understand what it would take to be successful. Unfortunately, there weren't many that looked, sounded, or acted like me at the top. But that didn't stop me from learning and paving the way while never compromising my true authenticity. Today, I'm happy to say I made a name for myself in the industry and continue to pave the way.

Throughout my journey, I never forgot the foundation that has shaped me and my success—my familia. As a Latina, I understood the power of love and the support of my loved ones. Latinidad is more than just food and music; it is a bond that keeps us grounded through our ups and downs. My family became my biggest cheerleaders, celebrating every milestone I achieved—like the purchase of my own home, paying for my own wedding, every promotion in my career, etc. They were my purpose and the reason why I never gave up.

Today, my passion is centered around diversity and inclusion and in creating a more equitable world. I aim to lift others up during the process, so others don't have to feel alone as they navigate their own journeys. Most importantly, I use my voice to speak up against injustice and advocate for those who may feel unheard. My goal is to continue to empower our Latinx community to unite and help one another, because together we can achieve much greatness.

I'll end by saying, "Never compromised your authentic self, keep pushing through the odds while always remembering to inspire and lift others up along the way"

BIOGRAPHY

Monique Le is the Managing Director and Head of iShares Digital Wealth and Individual Investor Business (DW&I). She is responsible for shaping the strategy and execution of commercial priorities for the largest and fastest growing US wealth channel. Monique focuses on servicing digital investment platforms and non-financial brands looking to launch investment products. She also manages strategic partnerships and scaled distribution to increase market share for iShares. Additionally, Monique is dedicated to building iShares' relationship with individual investors and has developed key brand programs to empower investors with the tools and knowledge they need. Monique brings over a decade of experience in brand building and business strategy to her role. She is also a strong advocate for diversity and inclusion and serves as the Global Co-Chair of the firm's SOMOS Latinx Employee Network. Monique holds a Bachelor of Science in Business Administration from Seton Hall University and resides in Jersey City with her family.

THE ASTONISHING LIGHT OF YOUR OWN BEING

MAYOLA LEAL

"I wish I could show you, when you are lonely or in darkness, the astonishing light of your own being."

On a magical day in May 2019, my husband and I found ourselves celebrating our fifth anniversary in the captivating city of Paris. The air was infused with joy and love as we walked hand in hand through the beautiful streets, and it was amidst the enchanting atmosphere that we made a momentous decision—to start a family.

During our trip, we stumbled upon a quaint bookstore where a certain phrase caught my eye: "I wish I could show you, when you are lonely and in darkness, the astonishing light of your own being." These words resonated with me deeply and became a guiding light during my journey into motherhood, which soon unfolded amidst a pandemic.

Nine months later, back in New York, we joyfully welcomed a beautiful girl into our lives in February 2020. However, our happiness was met with the grim reality of the world. The city that never sleeps became the epicenter of a pandemic, and the bustling streets turned eerily quiet. Fear and uncertainty permeated the air, as rising infection rates and overwhelmed hospitals dominated every conversation. It felt as though darkness had cast its shadow over our lives, and loneliness settled deep within our hearts.

As new parents, our primary concern was to safeguard the health and well-being of our daughter. We isolated ourselves from friends and family, navigating the challenges of parenthood in solitude. Being a proud Mexican, raised in a culture where family holds paramount importance, the physical distance from my loved ones during this crucial time intensified my feelings of loneliness.

Amidst the chaos and uncertainty, the profound quote became my guiding mantra. It served as a reminder that even in the darkest moments, an astonishing light resides within me. When loneliness and doubt loomed large, I drew upon this inner light to illuminate my path and guide me through the challenges I faced.

I immersed myself in the role of motherhood, cherishing every precious moment with my daughter. Within the confines of our home, we created a cocoon of love and safety. We sang, danced, and laughed together, finding solace in the simplicity of these shared experiences. In those intimate moments, I discovered an unyielding resilience and a boundless capacity for love within myself.

Through the darkness, I also witnessed the light of humanity and the unwavering support of my family. Communities came together, offering solace and solidarity. Family events kept us connected, even if held virtually. The sound of pots and pans clashing together filled our spirits every evening at 7 p.m. We realized that we were not alone in our fears and anxieties and that the collective strength of human kindness had the power to conquer even the darkest of times.

In the end, this transformative experience has forged me into a stronger and more resilient individual. But the unlock of it all was the light of my own being. To those who find themselves in a moment of loneliness or darkness, let that light guide you, remind your innate strength, and illuminate the world to bring us closer together.

BIOGRAPHY

Proudly born and raised In Mexico, Mayola Leal also considers herself a citizen of the world thanks to a collection of global life and work experiences, from Mexico City to New Zealand, Dallas, and now New York. She anchors her life's choices in five core values: integrity, family, respect, resiliency, and curiosity. Her desire to improve the world, combined with her natural inclination for curiosity, led her to pursue a degree in industrial engineering to leave a positive impact and the world a better place for her children.

FLOR LEIBASCHOFF

"Instead of being deterred by NOs, get ON a solution to turn the tables. And remember, when we read NO backward, it transforms into ON."

In a world that expects positivity, embracing NOs may seem contradictory.

However, to unlock our true potential, we must conquer challenges.

My South American heritage fuels this belief; blame it on that!

Life comes with obstacles; we are urged to come to the world, pushing us away from our comfort zone. The professional realm is no exception. As a female leader, I learned that to have a say, we must push ourselves through uncomfortable situations, too. Latinas in the United States represent less than 1 percent of leading positions. Only two chief commercial officers (CCOs) represent the $1.9 trillion United States Hispanic (USH) market, with more than twenty agencies! Some argue there's progress. It remains slow.

We still have people who don't want to share the cover photo. I just encountered such a situation. The female photographer told them to give me some space. Change can happen. It takes work. And togetherness.

We need to get from NO sharing to we'll be ON this committee. Stop asking permission. Instead, speak up with intention. If you are a minority of the minority, I get it, it's exhausting. But being part of something bigger is rewarding.

- So go ON; demand to be recognized for talent, not just gender.
- Don't be passive. Be intentional in everything.
- Instead of being deterred by NOs, get ON a solution to turn the tables.
- Embrace mistakes, move forward.
- Taming egos and maintaining a long-term goal are essential. Persistence is key.
- The right person will acknowledge our worth.
- We are not made to fit every shoe, which is our greatness.

I recall my entry into advertising, devoid of connections. At nineteen, during a job interview in Argentina and eager for an agency opportunity, a media director interviewed me.

Media director: Do you like math?
Flor: Thanks for your time.

That taught me the importance of knocking on the right doors rather than countless ones.

See? Optimization is crucial in all aspects of life. Fast forward twenty-five years, and I'm writing as an agency CCO from an awarded up-and-coming agency en route to the Cannes Lions International Festival of Creativity. Recently, many questioned the significance of the awards industry. For me, it provides visibility— showcasing our creative mindset. We learn from peers, celebrate achievements, and find inspiration. Plus, it gives young, talented Latinas hope that even as the minority of the minority, we can roar, too.

As the first Latina representing the US Hispanic market at the Cannes Young Creatives Competition (winning a Silver Lion), we had nothing to lose except ego. Fear of rejection served as powerful motivation. That and our creative director's words, "Don't come back if you don't win." Ironically those were his words the first time we met.

- Rejection was a constant companion throughout our journey, as in this career.
- Most of our ideas are born to be killed, all in pursuit of a better one.
- And remember, when we read NO backwards, it transforms into ON.
- ON to greatness.
- ON to unleashing that fire we were born with.
- From NO to ONwards.

BIOGRAPHY

Flor Leibaschoff has a thing for ideas. She is a passionate storyteller and was the first Hispanic female Chief Creative Officer in the USH. She has been named Shining Star by the American Advertising Federation and Woman to Watch by DMN (Data. Strategy. Technology), NY. After working in the industry for over twenty years, Flor co-founded and leads BeautifulBeast as CCO. BeautifulBeast is a business growth company dedicated to cross-cultural solutions through creativity and big data. A pioneer in the industry, the first YC with a Silver Lion, and former Círculo Creativo USA president acting on the Board of Directors.

BE GENEROUS WITH PEOPLE WHO ARE LESS FORTUNATE

LEXI LOPEZ

"Be generous with people who are less fortunate because philanthropy feeds your heart and spirit and gives more purpose to your work."

I grew up in Elizabeth, New Jersey, born to a Puerto Rican mother and Ecuadorian father. I was one of five children, raised in a faith-filled humble home. Growing up in a Catholic home, I learned from a young age that community service is a responsibility that we each should have. Giving to others and sharing with those less fortunate was something very important to my family.

Community service comes in various forms. I saw firsthand how my father gave of his time, especially to our church family. He would lead Bible classes on Friday evenings. He also served as a Lector, Eucharistic Minister, and as a Catechist. He loved talking and sharing his faith, and to this day, at seventy-seven years young, he takes the time to share with me anything that may have inspired him that day because of faith. I learned from my father that serving our church community was a way to give to back. I have followed his footsteps and I've raised my hand and use my voice to share the good word and share love by serving as a catechist and help to prepare our youth for their sacraments. This kind of community service is giving of your time, sharing faith filled inspiration, and being a light to others.

Philanthropy is a great way to give more purpose to one's life, to fulfill one's heart and souls. We can give back to our communities by not only volunteering of our time but helping existing charitable organizations or setting them up to help raise awareness of a cause. There are so many ways to give back, such as serving in a soup kitchen, mentoring a child, donating books or clothes, or visiting the elderly.

In 2019, I became a National Association of Hispanic Real Estate Professionals (NAHREP) 10 Certified Trainer. NAHREP and the Hispanic Wealth Project created the NAHREP 10 Wealth Disciplines to help others understand wealth and set realistic financial goals that would lead to generational wealth building. One of their disciplines is as follows: Be generous with people who are less fortunate because philanthropy feeds your heart and spirit and gives more purpose to your work.

As a final thought, I share the following words that Salesian Priest Alfonso Francia once said, "Nada que se da, se pierde. Siempre en mejor mano esta, cuando esta en la que recibe que cuando esta en la que se da." ("Nothing that is given, is lost. It is always in a better hand when it is in the one that receives than when it is in the one that is given.")

There's so much joy and pleasure in giving back to our communities!

I welcome you to follow my life journey, both personal and professional, via various social media platforms, such as Facebook (https://www.facebook.com/lexilou1206), Instagram (Lexi. Lopez.1206) and LinkedIn (https://www.linkedin.com/in/lexilopez-7a0295a/)

BIOGRAPHY

Lexi Lopez is a Senior Manager of Awards and Recognition with Century 21 Real Estate, LLC (Anywhere brand) where she assists brokers and agents with reports and tools to track transaction production, as well as manage the system's customer satisfaction survey program. Lexi knows how important it is to be a team player, inspirer, and motivator, on both a professional and personal level. Lexi is a National Association of Hispanic Real Estate Professionals (NAHREP) 10 Certified Trainer, where she delivers the important ten disciplines for anyone to adopt to lead healthier financial and personal lives. Lexi is also a Board of Director member since 2021 for the Cornerstone Family Programs (https://cornerstonefamilyprograms.org/) and Morristown Neighborhood House, which serve diverse minority communities throughout Morris County, New Jersey.

EMPOWERING MY INNER 'WILD THING'

CLARA LUCIO

"I learned to reframe confusing parallel identities as a richer, more expansive, and more meaningful sense of self."

Like many young and promising Latinas, I was a "community project." Deemed young, bright, and full of potential, my community invested in me to "hechar a la nena pa'lante" (roughly translates to "push this girl forward"). I used to wonder how I became one. While I was intelligent, quick, and socially adept, I was also immature, loud, messy, and impulsive. They used to call me "wild thing." Like many community kids, I lived parallel realities. By day, I went to an American private school full of Puerto Rico's wealthiest kids. After school, I'd head to my grandparent's house in a federal housing complex.

The homework I was given rivaled that of America's poshest private elementary schools, but my answers were checked by my grandmother, who couldn't read English. My mother would often arrive after a long day's work to realize I had painted the cat blue instead of red. I did this partly because I didn't understand the instructions and partly because I didn't want to understand them. In my teens, I was diagnosed with ADHD, and a lifelong dance with my brain began. I learned to train it, to negotiate with it, and to regulate it. As I grew, I wanted to make good on my community's investment in me. I was a champion debater at Yale and forged a successful career in the years after graduation. I was, by all intents and purposes, a successful adult.

The pressure to build on that momentum grew as my success grew. My community had supplied me with endless love and support; they had unknowingly poured many generations' worth of unrealized wants and expectations into me. My parents' careers also grew. With that, so did my resources and my access to opportunities. I had no excuse. They had done more with less. How could I not do more with more?

The pressure made me lose my way several times. I felt no real sense of identity. Winning and pleasing became what I was good at. I struggled with food bingeing, alcohol abuse, and Adderall addiction. Over time, I started making a helpful connection. Learning to deal with my ADHD forced me to prioritize my relationship with my brain and do that daily. David Foster Wallace famously said critical thinking is the ability to "consciously decide what has meaning and what doesn't." The coping mechanisms I had developed to function and not let others down also had made me an exceptional critical thinker.

I started to reframe almost every aspect of my life. If I carried several generations' worth of unlived expectations, I would have to figure out what to pay attention to and what to ignore, or I would drown. It meant reframing what often had been confusing parallel identities as a richer, more expansive, and more meaningful sense of self.

I still carry my community with me in my life, head, and heart, but I am more selective in what I choose to take forward. It is an ongoing, evolving process that includes owning that inner loud, impetuous, and messy "wild thing." I wouldn't be who or where I am without her.

BIOGRAPHY

Clara Alejandra Lucio, a brand marketer, crafts impactful stories through content communication and experiential campaigns. She kickstarted her career at PepsiCo and Fusion-an ABC and Univision Joint Venture, leading editorial, business development, and consumer marketing efforts. Clara earned accolades, including EPPY and D&AD awards for media work. With a focus on social impact startups, she excels in overseeing marketing and communications teams. Her branding efforts for impact-driven brands led to triple-digit engagement growth and millions of views and downloads. Born and raised in San Juan, Puerto Rico, Clara holds a Bachelor of Arts Degree from Yale University in religious studies and political science. She is passionate about dancing, cardio boxing, mezcal drinks, and Puerto Rico's socioeconomic progress.

CHANGING A LIFE

LUZ MAGAÑA

"I have evolved into the woman I was destined to be."

At the age of seventeen, I was undocumented, unemployable, terrified, and a new mother. Something had to change, if not for me, then for my son. Loving my baby boy would change his life, and I accepted the thought that I may never fulfill my dream of earning a college degree.

A few years later, my daughter was born. My family was my life. I was happy being at home with my children but felt restless. I still wanted a college education, but my fears were seeming insurmountable. Over ten years had passed since I was in a classroom. My command of English remained limited, and I feared not having the money to pay for tuition or books because my immigration status prohibited me from working.

Still, over the years, I held onto my dream. Then one day, the president of the United States signed an executive order that granted approximately 800,000 immigrants limited protected status. The

Deferred Action for Childhood Arrivals (DACA) allowed people like me to work, study, and live in the country without fear of deportation.

This moved me to do something bold, so I enrolled as a full-time student at a local community college. I was so excited about the opportunity! But the excitement soon waned when I realized how challenging college coursework was and its unaffordability. I applied for many private scholarships to help defray the cost of an associate degree.

As much as I wanted a college education, I felt foolish and inadequate for returning to school at this point in my life. Many times, my ten-year-old son helped me with my writing assignments. Yes, my little boy literally became my college English tutor.

One day, I felt overburdened. My five-year-old daughter caught me crying at the kitchen table and urged me not to quit school. The encouragement and support of this small child helped me overcome my self-doubts and fears. She kept me going. It took me three years of hard work and many sacrifices to earn my degree, but I did. I graduated Magna Cum Laude. Imagine that!

Thanks to my college education and sheer determination, I was given the opportunity to work as a finance coordinator for the United States Hispanic Leadership Institute (USHLI), one of the largest Hispanic advocacy groups in the country. I helped families and students in preparing for college and in organizing and conducting its national conference, attended annually by 6,000 present and future leaders representing 40 states. USHLI has changed tens of thousands of lives.

A few years later, with the support of my family, dear mentors, and God, I decided to pursue a Bachelor's Degree. Finding time to keep up with school and home responsibilities while fulfilling my full-time job duties wasn't easy, but I did it and graduated with highest distinction!

My story is short, but it is certainly not over. The best is yet to come. Going back to school was a life-changing experience for me. I now realize that it meant more than earning a college degree. Along the way, I discovered something new. I discovered myself. I discovered that I am someone special, that I matter, and am no longer scared or insecure. I have evolved into the woman I was destined to be—a leader in her community—and realized that I achieved the dream of my seventeen-year-old self was to change a life . . . and the life that changed was my own!

BIOGRAPHY

Luz Magaña migrated to the United States from Mexico City at a very young age. A DACA recipient, she is the first in her family to graduate college, Luz has dedicated most of her professional career to motivating students to reach their potential by pursuing post-secondary education or training.

Previously, Luz helped organize and conduct the largest Hispanic leadership conference in the nation and is currently the Executive Director of Hispanic Serving Institution Initiatives at a university. Luz hopes that her story inspires others to take advantage of all opportunities to better themselves and advance the community.

BRIDGING CULTURES: MY JOURNEY
TO CREATE INCLUSIVE SPACES
FOR SPANISH SPEAKERS IN THE
MIDWEST

PAOLA MARIZÁN

"You see, like millions of people currently living in the United States, I grew up bilingual. My brain automaticamente moves between languages and so my thought is WHY CAN'T OUR CONTENT ALSO BE THAT WAY?"

When I first arrived in the Midwest from Puerto Rico, it was an overwhelming culture shock. I searched high and low, couldn't find sofrito or plantains, and Spanish seemed to be vanished from the conversations around me. Of course, I understood that I was no longer in Puerto Rico, but Spanish speakers were here, too.

After completing my journalism degree, I joined WNIN, the local public radio station in Evansville, Indiana. While my colleagues were warm and welcoming, I didn't feel adequately represented by the content being produced on air. Whenever a Spanish speaker appeared in a news story, their voice would be muffled by a voiceover.

"Y cuando eso pasó, me sentí presionado" (fades out) . . . "José says when this happened, he felt pressured to make the change."

In my ideal world, Spanish and English stood on equal footing. Determined to address this issue, I approached my supervisor and, to my surprise, he shared the same concern and asked me to incorporate Spanish into my on-air segments. The audience's response was overwhelmingly positive. But I knew it wasn't enough. I longed to say more than "Hola, mi nombre es Paola Marizán— and you're listening to 88.3 FM." I aspired to say, "Hola, mi nombre es Paola Marizán—and you're listening to 88.3 FM, la estación que te trae the best of news, right here. Quedaté con nosotros."

You see, I grew up bilingual. My mind effortlessly transitions between languages, prompting me to question why our content couldn't do the same. I began pitching stories that not only embraced English but also celebrated Spanish. I aimed to narrate tales about the Puerto Rican diaspora, shed light on Mexican families struggling to make ends meet, and highlight the flourishing Cuban entrepreneurs. By sharing these stories and experiences in their own languages, I hoped to unite the Latino and Hispanic communities.

This journey was far from easy. Some colleagues pushed back, deeming the inclusion of more Spanish unnecessary. However, I refused to let their skepticism deter me. I knew there was an audience hungry for this type of content. That's when *Qué Pasa, Midwest?* was born—a bilingual podcast and WhatsApp newsletter dedicated to sharing the stories of Latine individuals in the Midwest.

Gradually, I began to witness change. Our audience expanded, and I received heartfelt messages from people grateful to hear stories in their native language. We started inviting more Spanish-speaking guests to our shows, and bilingual interviews became the norm.

From that point forward, my mission became clear: to ensure that our station, as well as others, produced inclusive and representative content that mirrored the community we served. Over the course of five years, I tirelessly advocated for bilingual content and assisted numerous stations across the United States in hiring bilingual reporters and producers. Together, we expanded coverage to include diverse voices and perspectives.

Today, I take great pride in saying that WNIN is a station that embraces diversity and inclusion. I am immensely grateful to have used my voice to create more inclusive spaces for Spanish speakers in the Midwest. It is my hope that my work will inspire others to do the same—to seamlessly transition from language to language, never missing a beat.

BIOGRAPHY

Paola Marizán is a Dominican journalist who made it her mission to create more inclusive spaces for Spanish speakers in the Midwest. After experiencing a culture shock when she first arrived in the Midwest, Paola joined WNIN, a local public radio station, where she realized the lack of Spanish representation in their content. She pitched bilingual stories and successfully brought in more Spanish-speaking guests to their shows, which led to the creation of the bilingual podcast and WhatsApp newsletter, *Qué Pasa, Midwest?* Paola's advocacy for bilingual content has helped multiple stations around the United States to hire more bilingual reporters and producers and expand their coverage to include more diverse voices and perspectives.

MAURICIO MARTINEZ

"Let's keep living, loving and let's keep singing."

"Life can change so quickly" are words I sang eight times a week for almost two years in a beautiful musical that made one of my biggest dreams come true: starring on Broadway. Those words resonate with me to this day.

In the summer of 2018, I was living my dream: I sold out my 54 Below debut in New York City and, a week later, I was opening On Your Feet! The Story of Gloria & Emilio Estefan. On a Saturday morning in Los Angeles (LA), a recurring nightmare returned.

When you're a cancer survivor, the word "tumor" becomes a part of your vocabulary but not something you want to hear ever again. I began my battle against bladder cancer in 2010. The day I opened the show in LA, I was a three-time cancer survivor. A month later, I became a four time cancer survivor.

If I were to describe the feeling, I would quote a dear friend who told me, "You were hit by a tsunami; you need time to feel the pain, heal the wounds, stand up and start all over again." That is exactly what I did. I needed time to reflect, recover and recharge. There was a lot to process.

After some time off, I chose to share this personal matter for two reasons.

First and most importantly, maybe someone out there is thinking of giving up. In that case, read this and feel hope. Yes, life can be scary sometimes. And yes, cancer sucks. BIG TIME. But life also can be beautiful. I know this first hand. It's that imperfect balance that makes you appreciate the good things and learn from the not-so-good ones.

Second, I now see all of this as a blessing rather than a curse. It's important to count one's blessings. This is a blessing because the tumors were low grade and were found very early. Today, I am cancer free again. I am fortunate to have an incredible support system of family and loved ones, and I'm in great medical hands. I am alive, healthy and loved . . . and nothing is more important than that.

Finally, this is a blessing because I have an amazing job that I look forward to doing for the rest of my life.

I returned to the stage of On Your Feet! and sang the words "life can change so quickly." Sometimes I would imagine that I sang that lullaby to myself as a child, as if I were telling my 7-year-old self, "It's gonna be alright. Everything is gonna be alright. The nightmare is over."

I don't know if it's over, but July 2023 marked my first time passing the five-year mark cancer free. That feels like a miracle and is definitely why I feel so grateful. I've learned that, when faced with adversity, it's better not to run away. I assure you that, once you go through it, you will learn, grow and come out stronger. I hope this helps someone as it's helped me.

Let's keep living, loving and let's keep singing.

BIOGRAPHY

Mauricio Martínez is a Mexican Emmy-winning actor and recording artist known for his work in film, television, albums, concerts, plays, and musicals. He made his Broadway debut portraying Emilio Estefan in On Your Feet! and toured nationally, earning acclaim at prestigious venues like The Kennedy Center and The Pantages Theatre. Mauricio's talent shines in Mexico and Latin America with appearances in popular TV series and telenovelas. He has released two Latin pop albums and will record his sold-out, one-man show, 5'11, Based In NYC, in fall 2023. Mauricio's stage credits include Andrew Lloyd Webber's Unmasked and memorable performances in Man of La Mancha, Beauty and the Beast, and Saturday Night Fever. He also serves as a judge on the first season of RuPaul's Drag Race Mexico.

ELVIN MATOS

*"Grief and pain can be used as fuel to propel yourself forward
rather than hold yourself back."*

Losing a loved one is never easy, but losing two just months apart was an experience that shook me to the core. In 2018, I lost my husband, Stephen, to suicide; a few months later, my mother passed away from a sudden cardiac arrest. They were the two most important people in my life. I was left feeling alone, hopeless, and unsure about what to do next.

The months that followed were a blur of grief, confusion, regret, guilt, and anger. And there were days when I didn't want to get out of bed, let alone face the world outside.

But then an unexpected shift happened.

Stephen and my mom always believed in me. They saw something in me that I sometimes didn't see in myself, and their unwavering support and encouragement stayed with me long after they were gone. So, their memories became a catalyst for change in my life. I knew that I had to honor them in some way, to make them proud. I realized: Grief and pain can be used as fuel to propel yourself forward rather than hold yourself back.

The following year, I took a leap of faith and quit my job, a job that I was comfortable in, but one that didn't challenge me anymore. I decided to strengthen my skill set as a marketer and advance my career, not only to make Stephen and my mom proud but to represent Latinos in my field.

It felt like a reset. A chance to start fresh and build something new. I threw myself into learning and developing my skills, determined to become a stronger marketer. I started following and connecting with marketing thought leaders on LinkedIn. I attended free webinars and virtual events. And I started reading more books, such as *The End of Marketing* by Carlos Gil, *Everybody Writes* by Ann Handley, *Influence: The Psychology of Persuasion* by Robert B. Cialdini, PhD. and *The Adweek Copywriting Handbook* by Joseph Sugarman.

I'll admit there were times when I felt overwhelmed and doubted myself—my old friend imposter syndrome visited me from time to time—but I knew that giving up was never an option. Through my hard work and perseverance, I was able to double my salary and become a first-time homeowner. These achievements may seem small on their own, but they represent a much greater personal triumph: the triumph of resilience and determination in the face of overwhelming adversity.

BIOGRAPHY

Elvin Matos is a marketing professional with a Bachelor's Degree in Business Management from Golden Gate University. He specializes in helping staffing and recruitment companies with go-to-market strategies, growing market share, and driving brand consideration for potential clients and candidates. Elvin's skills in content creation, search engine optimization (SEO) and search engine marketing (SEM), social media, paid advertising, email marketing, design, and video production have helped him achieve a proven track record of success in the industry. Born and raised in San Francisco, he currently resides in Houston, Texas, where he continues to apply his marketing expertise to assist clients in achieving their business objectives.

RETURNING HOME

HILDA MCCLURE

"The most remarkable gift we can give ourselves is the freedom to embrace the parts of our culture that honor us and to release those that no longer serve us."

"Your culture won't matter in the Kingdom of God," my friend uttered to me while I shared my pain of not fitting in. While her intention was well-meaning, those words left a lasting impact on me. In that simple sentence, it felt as though my entire cultural identity was being stripped away.

Growing up in Puerto Rico with a Puerto Rican father and an American mother from New Jersey, I straddled two worlds. At home, we spoke English and Spanish, but outside, my reality revolved solely around Spanish. I resembled my father, but my speech mirrored my mother's. I delighted in dancing to Marc Anthony and the Gran Combo, yet I couldn't fathom having rice and beans every day of my life.

When I moved to Texas at the age of eighteen to attend a private Baptist university, I didn't expect to perpetually feel like a fish out of water. Despite being a US citizen and speaking impeccable English, I struggled to form meaningful connections. It always seemed as though I didn't quite fit in. I wrestled with God, seeking clarity on where I belonged, as I felt neither Latina enough nor white enough.

Then, one day, while sharing my pain with a friend, I heard her remark that unintentionally erased my cultural heritage. From that moment, I embarked on a journey of assimilation. Over the next decade, I gradually hid the Hispanic part of me in pursuit of acceptance. I began dressing like my friends, stopped listening to Marc Anthony and Calle 13, and disregarded many of my cultural roots.

Two years ago, I transitioned my career to serve my own comunidad alongside courageous Latinas. This choice became a transformative invitation to revive the dormant parts of myself—the Latina that had faded away in order to fit in. I found phenomenal women who understood the delicate dance of being Latina in the United States and embraced their culture unabashedly, all while talking Spanglish. Slowly but surely, I found myself embracing the rhythms of Bad Bunny, wearing red lipstick reminiscent of my tias, and embodying my Papi's hospitality by welcoming others in my home. In doing so, I felt a profound sense of homecoming within my body, a connection that had been absent.

I soon realized that I had not only rediscovered my cultural identity but also returned home to myself. I began carving out more space for my heritage in my daily life, allowing it to take up all the space it needed in me. We, a people of two cultures, live in the in-between, which is beautiful. However, we often face pressure to fit into one or the other. Yet, the most remarkable gift we can give ourselves is the freedom to embrace the parts of our culture that honor us and release those that no longer serve us. Just as we decorate our home to reflect ourselves, we must do the same within us, granting space to every part that longs to be seen, heard, and loved.

BIOGRAPHY

Hilda McClure is the Chief Operating Officer (COO) at Cannenta Center for Healing and Empowerment, specializing in trauma-focused counseling and early childhood education. She is a licensed professional Counselor Associate, trained eye movement desensitization and reprocessing (EMDR) Therapist and Somatic Experiencing Practitioner in training. Hilda has developed evidence-based interventions for children, authored articles on trauma and childhood development, and presented on psychology theories and modalities for professionals. She is dedicated to sharing her knowledge with other professionals to increase their skillset and help others. Hilda holds a Master of Arts in Counseling and a Bachelor of Science in Early Childhood Education.

THE POWER OF FAMILIA

CARLOS MEDINA

"Relationships are today's new currency."—*Ted Rubin*

Growing up, my father, Modesto Medina, instilled in me the importance of relationships. With just five dollars and a dream, he fled Cuba, facing numerous obstacles along the way. However, it was his charm and ability to form meaningful connections that helped him overcome adversity. His teachings on the value of relationships would become a guiding force in my own life.

Dad fled Cuba and came to the Tri-State area. He served in the United States Army during the Korean War which provided his citizenship and a path to the prestigious New York Times where he worked for over forty years. While at the Times Modesto helped dozens of Hispanic gain employment at the paper. He started the Hispanic Society, Cooking Club, and other employee resource groups at the times. Always helping others and developing relationships.

Over a decade ago, I found myself at a crossroads when

the Statewide Hispanic Chamber of Commerce of New Jersey (SHCCNJ) was in crisis. Our founder fell ill, leaving us with a debt of over $300,000, and creditors were closing in. Instead of running away, I decided to face the challenge head-on, armed with the power of relationships and my father's teachings in my head.

I wholeheartedly embraced the belief of my friend, Ted Rubin, that relationships are the currency of today's world. In this context, I redefined relationships as "Familia"—individuals who are close to you, have your back, and provide unwavering support. They are not jealous but offer positive words of encouragement, both in your presence and when speaking about you to others.

Drawing upon the strength of my Familia, I embarked on the journey to turn the chamber around. I reached out to trusted allies, influential community leaders, and dedicated members who believed in our mission. Through their support, guidance, and unwavering belief in me, we navigated the treacherous waters and began rebuilding the chamber from the ground up.

The transformation of the SHCCNJ stands as a testament to the power of Familia and the importance of relationships. It was through these connections that we were able to mend broken partnerships, secure crucial sponsorships, and reestablish trust within the community. The chamber flourished, becoming a beacon of support and opportunity for Hispanic businesses in New Jersey.

My father's lessons on the value of relationships were invaluable in this journey. His ability to form genuine connections taught me that, in times of crisis, it is the strength of our relationships that will carry us forward. By nurturing and cherishing our Familia, we create a network of unwavering support that propels us toward success.

In the end, my story is a testament to the fact that relationships, or Familia, are indeed today's new currency. It is through these bonds that we find solace, support, and the encouragement needed to overcome even the most daunting challenges. As we invest in our relationships and foster a culture of trust and positivity, we unlock limitless possibilities for personal and professional growth.

BIOGRAPHY

Carlos Medina is a devoted advocate for the Hispanic community, notably as President of the Statewide Hispanic Chamber of Commerce of New Jersey. His efforts have been crucial in promoting diversity in entrepreneurship and recognizing the invaluable contributions of Hispanic-owned businesses. Carlos's commitment extends to serving on various non-profit boards, empowering entrepreneurs from diverse backgrounds. He has received recognition for his philanthropy, including the Jefferson Medal, and has been chosen as a college commencement speaker thrice. As the leader of Robinson Aerial, Carlos displays exceptional leadership skills. Additionally, his role as Executive Producer and Host of the popular PBS show, *Que Pasa*, underscores his dedication to fostering awareness and understanding among a broad audience.

IGNITING RESILIENCE:
TRANSFORMING ADVERSITY INTO
MASTERPIECES

MARIA MEDRANO

"My story is not about overcoming obstacles—it's about transforming adversity into opportunity and using my experiences to create positive change."

I was born to a teenage mom, an orphan, who believed wholeheartedly that with her love, I would change our family's outlook. For that, I am eternally grateful. This is the beginning of my story, a story that I continue to write today with determination and resilience.

As the oldest and only daughter in my Mexican-American family, I naturally took on the roles of provider, caretaker, and leader from a young age. School became my world—a place where I could grow academically and witnessed the joy it brought my mom. Her smile and warm embrace were all the motivation I needed to work hard to change my family's outlook. My idea of providing went beyond tangible things; it encompassed learning new skills, sharing knowledge, building relationships, and earning money.

One vivid memory stands out from my childhood. I desperately wanted to be a part of the school baking club, although I knew deep down that we didn't have an oven. My wise mother taught me the value of finding alternate ways to contribute. Unable to bake, I took charge of organizing the club's sale, drawing upon my experience in coordinating my mom's bookkeeping tasks. I handled money with ease while capturing people's attention to influence more baking sales through my Español, "se vende pastelitos." These transferable skills, often possessed by first-generation, low-income students, are our superpowers. They are skills forged through the challenges of life and should be celebrated and recognized when pursuing job opportunities. I see this clearly now, but it was something I had to learn through trials and tribulations. When you are the first in your family to navigate uncharted paths, guidance is scarce, and the journey is lonely. I anchored myself in my upbringing and rejoiced in the memory of my mom's smile when I accomplished something new. This joy, born out of our limited resources, became a driving force throughout college and two decades in the corporate world. The ability to persist and remain resilient, despite the exhaustion, held deep meaning because I learned and proudly shared that my differences coupled with the solid foundation laid by my mom propelled me forward, always.

My story is not about overcoming obstacles—it's about transforming adversity into opportunity and using my experiences to create positive change. I am here to inspire others to embrace their unique backgrounds and circumstances, recognizing the strengths that come from facing challenges head-on. In the face of doubt and limited guidance, know you are resilient, and with persistence, will always succeed. It was the unwavering belief that a single person can ignite the flames of transformation, that propelled me towards a better future. I constantly reflect on the bake sale day, the day my entrepreneur spirit was unleashed. Today, you will find that spirit leading Inspírame. Whether you are the first in your family to carve a new path or faced with the challenges that life presents, remember that your story is far from finished. Your story, like my story, is still being written. Together, let's create masterpieces that inspire the world.

BIOGRAPHY

Maria Medrano, Co-Founder and Chief Executive Officer (CEO) of Inspirame, fights to improve educational experiences across disadvantaged communities. Thriving at the intersection of education, technology, and equitable outcomes, Maria is a balanced blend of business strategist and community advocate who served in senior diversity leadership roles with Google, Visa, and Cisco Systems. As a first-generation Mexican American, Maria is the first in her family to earn a high school or college degree. Additional accolades include Top 100 Under 40 Diversity MBA, Silicon Valley 40 Under 40, Top 50 Under 50, and YWCA Tribute to Women Emerging Leader Award.

DREAM BIG, DREAMING SMALL
COSTS THE SAME

TITO MELEGA

"When you care the most, you can't help but do your best. Let that be your gift to the world."

I grew up in Bragado, a rural city in Argentina that was named after the legend of a wild horse that chose death over slavery by jumping into the raging waters of the Bragado Lagune. This story has significantly influenced the values that I hold dear in my life.

As a teenager, I wasn't interested in team sports. Instead, I was drawn to a more romantic lifestyle filled with music, film, writing, drawing, and conversation.

However, I did manage to join our city's rugby team, where I was told to grab the ball, pick a flag, and run like hell, which was all I could manage with some level of competency.

Like many eighteen-year-old Argentines, I packed my dreams and moved to Buenos Aires searching for a future in a creative field like filmmaking or architecture.

There, I entered a vibrant new world inhabited by filmmakers, poets, and painters. A time and place where my "dreamer" mentality truly fit. However, it was all too short-lived.

First, my father passed of a sudden unexpected stroke.

Then, hyperinflation hit, hard.

You could spend twenty-five minutes wandering the aisles of the local market only to find out at the register that the prices had gone up. Like El Caballo De Bragado, I had a choice to make: I could face the possibility of becoming a burden on my hard-working mother or take flight and gamble that one day I could be the one doing the helping.

That's how I found myself at Miami International Airport with everything I owned in a backpack, eleven words of English, and $200 in my pocket. My next stop was Columbus, Indiana, where a wonderful family opened their door and treated me like a son.

With their help, I learned a new language, got my first job, and graduated with distinction from my first vocational college, which provided the springboard I needed to succeed.

The journey that followed was never easy, but I experienced great pride and accomplishment. From being a Junior Art Director, I rose to become a Global Chief Creative Officer, leading award-winning work for one of the world's largest advertising accounts. Mistakes were made. Learnings where learned. And, accolades, awards, and a purposeful life followed.

I also became a husband, a father, and an ally.

Although I am proud of everything I have achieved, what I'm even more proud of is never forgetting the values and beliefs I learned back at the shores of Bragado's lagune.

Here's where I must take a moment to recognize my mother, Mirta Aliano, one of the bravest women I know, who taught me to live each day guided by the philosophy of "caring the most." It's a principle that I apply in my daily life, whether it's at work or in my personal relationships.

Part of caring the most is doing my part to open the doors for others, championing equality in all its forms, and taking the time to reflect and never forget where I came from.

BIOGRAPHY

Tito Melega is a Chief Creative Officer, Executive Producer, and entrepreneur. Born in Argentina, he lives in the United States, where he's actively developing the moonshot female equality deserves, an act so bold it will inspire the world, much like NASA's Apollo 11's mission did in its time. Tito founded and curated TEDxHollywood, RisingUnited.org, wehustl3.com, and amaskforall.com. He advocates for Autism awareness, women's equality, and diversity in the workplace. His work features some of the most innovative advertising and brand experiences to date and resides in the permanent archives of the New York's Museum of Modern Art (MoMA) and National Museum of American History.

DAVID MOLFA

"My story reflects the promising potential that can be unleashed among Hispanic youth if there were more investment in outreach initiatives."

Growing up in Bushwick, Brooklyn, enriched me with its cultural and ethnic diversity, uplifted me with the pride and joyfulness characteristic of the Hispanic community, and reaffirmed my identity as an Afro-Latino-Dominican American. Notwithstanding the enriching pluralism of my social milieu, late in my high school years, I learned of a disheartening reality: the lack of educational investment for black and brown youth reared in Bushwick. Without some fortuitous encounters and flashes of serendipity, my academic achievements would have been limited and I would have suffered the same fate as my closest friends—not attending college, not recognizing my talents, and relying on illicit dealings to make some money. My story reflects the promising potential that can be unleashed among Hispanic youth if there were more investment in outreach initiatives.

My sophomore year of high school marked another unremarkable time when I was disinterested academically, received subpar grades, and had no concrete academic or professional aspirations. I was frequently absent and tardy, showing up to morning classes and leaving early right before lunch to hang out with friends. My interests were in fact centered on basketball, fashion, parties with friends, and chasing women.

Everything changed when my teachers took pity on me and tried to rescue my academic career by placing me in the Committee for Hispanic Children and Families (CHCF) Young Men's Leadership Program. It gave talented but struggling students experiential learning opportunities through a series of workshops that exposed participants to college and career options. The program had curricula that sparked impassioned discussions about our community and the injustices engulfing it. Not only did the transformative internship kindle my academic inquisitiveness, but it also taught me how to be a professional.

Before the internship, CHCF furnished me with the necessary professional attire ranging from colorful ties and shoes to blazers and slacks. Wearing these suits felt good but not for the superficial reasons relating to fashion. For I was engaging with like-minded professionals and thus expanding my network, and this made me realize how, by re-committing academically, I could become a successful professional in any realm. This is what I did for the next two years of high school as reflected by the immediate upswing of my GPA by the end of my senior year. This behavioral change continued into college, where I graduated with high honors in biology and sociology, and now I'm a second-year law student at St. John's University School of Law with the aspiration of becoming an attorney.

My encounter with CHCF might not have been necessary if there were a system in place to develop our Hispanic youth, especially those in underprivileged communities, to become productive members of society.

BIOGRAPHY

David Molfa is a 2024 Juris Doctor candidate at St. John's University School of Law. David obtained his Bachelor of Arts in Biology and Sociology, cum laude, from Queens College, City University of New York (CUNY), in 2020. After graduating, he taught math and science courses at his alma mater. After his first year of law school, David interned at an investment fund and volunteered at a nonprofit, helping immigrants with their visa applications. As a first-generation student, he draws inspiration from his working-class background to continue to be a voice for the underprivileged and underrepresented.

EMBRACING CHANGE: CATALYST FOR
TRANSFORMATION AND GROWTH

VANESSA MONTAÑEZ

"Without change, there would be no butterflies. Let us embrace change and become the transformative force that the world needs."

"Embracing change: Catalyst for transformation and growth." This inspiring quote resonates deeply with me. "Without change, there would be no butterflies. Let us embrace change and become the transformative force that the world needs."

Born and raised in Los Angeles, California, I come from a close-knit family of Mexican heritage. Being the eldest among four siblings, I was instilled with a strong appreciation for education from an early age. My parents, unable to pursue their own higher education, impressed upon us the immense value of learning. Privileged to attend private schools, I recognized the pivotal role education plays in shaping a brighter future, fostering professional growth, and driving socioeconomic advancement. Particularly in the United States, where social and economic stratification persists, education remains a potent differentiator.

Within this context, it is heartening to witness the rising prominence of Latinas, particularly millennial Latinas, who are increasingly pursuing higher education, attaining associate, bachelor's, and graduate degrees, and beyond. I firmly believe that anyone can achieve greatness when they wholeheartedly invest their passion and perseverance.

My professional journey has led me to a successful career in mortgage lending, marked by significant achievements and managerial advancements. However, a few years ago, I encountered an unforeseen setback when my regional position was eliminated, resulting in my first layoff. Ascending the career ladder becomes increasingly challenging as one reaches higher echelons. In response, I made the conscious decision to return to school, utilizing this transitional period to pursue a doctoral degree. My primary motivation was to immerse myself in a subject I genuinely enjoyed. I had previously acquired a Bachelor's and Master's Degree in Business, driven by the desire for career progression. During the years of 2007 to 2009, our nation experienced the profound impact of the Great Recession, triggered by the collapse of the housing bubble. As the economy plummeted, blame was often attributed to real estate professionals and lenders. However, I held a deeper understanding, recognizing that the crisis stemmed from flawed leadership and unbridled greed. Consequently, I resolved to explore the realm of Executive Leadership, eager to study the principles of effective leadership as exemplified by executives. While there are numerous economic factors contributing to the Great Recession at its core, the calamity was a consequence of woeful management practices and an insatiable pursuit of personal gain.

As the first member of my family to pursue higher education while working fulltime, I embarked on the challenging journey of attaining a Doctoral Degree, ultimately graduating with honors and boasting a perfect 4.0-grade point average. This audacious pursuit symbolized my unwavering commitment to achieving ambitious goals and embracing change, irrespective of age or circumstances. I firmly believe that the pursuit of knowledge should be a paramount priority, advocating that all individuals consider returning to academia to acquire their degrees. By taking this proactive step, we not only evolve personally but also become catalysts for change, ensuring a brighter future for ourselves and inspiring others, particularly Latinas, to follow suit. Although the path may be arduous, we must persist with unwavering determination. It is through change that we unlock our true potential.

BIOGRAPHY

Vanessa Montañez, Senior Vice President and Community Lending National Sales Manager at City National Bank, oversees sales growth and manages an external mortgage sales team. With more than twenty-five years in residential lending, she previously held positions at US Bank, East West Bank, and JP Morgan Chase. Recognized as one of the Women of Influence: Finance by the Los Angeles Business Journal, Vanessa is the Chief Executive Officer and Co-founder of LeadHER talks and contributes to *Women's Mortgage Magazine*. Actively involved in the community, she serves on various boards and is a former President of the National Association of Hispanic Real Estate Professionals. Vanessa holds a Doctorate in executive leadership and a Master in Business Administration (MBA). Currently, she's authoring a book on social capital.

EMBRACE YOUR IDENTITY AND INSPIRE CHANGE

AMALIA MORENO-DAMGAARD

"Your journey can empower others to rise above barriers and create positive results."

I am a self-proclaimed double minority—a woman and an ethnic—within the Latino demographic majority in the United States. Rather than seeing this as a disadvantage, I embrace the strength of my minority identity. It empowers me to challenge stereotypes, break barriers, and pave the way for a more inclusive and equitable future. Through my work in media, I strive to highlight the diversity of Latin American culture in a positive, beautiful, and powerful way.

Overcoming my fears has been transformative. As a shy person, I used to fear having an accent, looking different, and speaking in public. But I refused to let those fears hold me back. I worked hard to conquer them, knowing that public speaking would give me visibility and a voice. This became instrumental in building my personal brand and career.

Growing up in Guatemala City, my parents' divorce led me to live with my maternal grandmother, Abuelita Mela. Despite the separation and my mother's abandonment, I chose to become a stronger woman rather than letting the pain hinder my dreams. Abuelita Mela, a divorced and self-sufficient woman, owned a variety store, where I often helped. Her business insight, thriftiness, social skills, and generosity taught me valuable entrepreneurial lessons. She also ignited my passion for cooking. Together, we visited the indigenous market, where I learned to appreciate high-quality ingredients. Abuelita Mela's artisanal cooking skills and ability to season well left a lasting impact on me. She became my North Star as an adult.

Moving to the United States, I initially pursued a career in international banking, following my sister's footsteps. Through various positions and banks, I gained business acumen and valuable experience. This knowledge became crucial when I transitioned to become a full-time entrepreneur, founding Amalia Latin Gourmet. As a Latina immigrant, I felt compelled to address misrepresentations of Latin American culture based on my own experience. My business mission became narrowing the awareness gap and promoting understanding and appreciation of Latin cultural nuances through traditional, healthy gourmet cuisine.

Co-founding Women Entrepreneurs of Minnesota, a nonprofit organization focused on fostering women entrepreneurship, diversity, and inclusion, has been rewarding. Serving on multiple nonprofit boards, including as the first Latina president of the National Association of Women Business Owners Minnesota

Chapter, allows me to give back, expand my network, build strategic relationships, and continue learning and growing.

Choosing to become an author further empowered me to amplify my voice. With two multi-award-winning books and a third in the works, I have been recognized by prestigious organizations, including Gourmand International. Through media appearances and writing in both languages, I aim to increase visibility and reach a wider audience.

In the kitchen, my true happy place, solace, and creativity converge. From there, I fulfill my purpose, mission, and vision to preserve cherished traditions and educate the world. With a clear purpose, my actions, decisions, and pursuits align with what truly matters, bringing harmony and fulfillment to my life.

I encourage everyone to find their purpose. When you set your mind to something and believe in your abilities, you have the potential to achieve incredible things. In a rapidly diversifying country, embracing self-empowerment, fostering equity and inclusion, and respecting cultural differences are key to creating a better future for all.

BIOGRAPHY

Guatemala native Amalia Moreno-Damgaard is a Le Cordon Bleu chef and founder of Amalia Latin Gourmet, and she empowers Fortune 500 brands to reach the Latino community's purchasing power. Through strategic consulting, speaking engagements, gourmet experiences, media collaborations, and acclaimed authorship, Amalia partners with renowned brands, like Betty Crocker Kitchens, Hormel Foods, Land O'Lakes, Crystal Farms, Target, Cargill, and 3M. She frequently appears on CBS *Mid-Morning, Fox 9 Good Day, Twin Cities Live,* Telemundo, and MPR's *All Things Considered,* also judging the PBS North Series, *The Great Minnesota Recipe.* Her award-winning books include *Amalia's Guatemalan Kitchen and Amalia's Mesoamerican Table.* Learn more at: AmaliaLatinGourmet.com.

ARACELY MORENO-MOSIER

"I try to build an environment where our voices will be heard, as well as a space for these individuals to develop their own voices. At work and in my community, I'm always making sure that I can be a voice for somebody. And to think it all started with an insult."

I grew up in a neighborhood on the south side of Fort Worth, Texas, that included many recent immigrants, most of whom struggled to get by. But because it was near an affluent neighborhood near the Texas Christian University (TCU) campus, my siblings and I attended schools with ample opportunities to fortify our minds and keep us out of trouble—honors programs, sports, and more.

Some of these required extra money, but my parents always found a way to pay, even if it meant foregoing other treats. After all, making sure their children had more opportunities was one of the reasons they came to this country.

But there were rewards, too. When I was in fifth grade, I won an academic student award, which came with a prize of four tickets to the local Six Flags. Since such a trip was beyond my parents' means, this was very exciting.

As fun as it was, what I remember most clearly from that day isn't any of the rides. Instead, it's a moment from when we were waiting in line. My little brother, bored and antsy, got into a minor scuffle with another boy, who was white. My parents weren't paying attention, but I saw the boy's mother move him away and heard her mutter to the father, "That little wetback was messing with him."

I was embarrassed—and angry. I didn't say anything to my parents for fear of escalating the situation—and I also was afraid of hurting them. But beyond the sting of the slur, I realized it showed the woman's ignorance. She didn't know that my family's history in this country dates back to the 1940s, when my abuelito came from Mexico to work here as part of a program to support the labor force while America was at war. After he returned home, his stories gave his children the confidence to immigrate here. They didn't know about the sacrifices my parents made because of their love for this country.

Right then, I decided I was going to be a voice for myself and others who have been insulted, silenced, and misunderstood. That moment propelled me to where I am now: a marketing executive at PepsiCo, one of the most recognizable companies in the world.

As a marketing leader, I make sure we listen to the power of the Hispanic consumer in the United States. As the executive sponsor of our ADELANTE Employee Resource Group, I also work to highlight Hispanic associates by providing professional opportunities for visibility and building allyship. As a board member for a local non-profit, I strive to empower others in South Dallas with the chances I had.

In these efforts, I try to build an environment where our voices will be heard, as well as a space for these individuals to develop their own voices. At work and in my community, I'm always making sure that I can be a voice for somebody. And to think it all started with an insult.

BIOGRAPHY

Aracely Moreno-Mosier is a classic first-generation Mexican American story. The first college graduate in her family, she worked for AT&T and Sara Lee before joining PepsiCo, where she now serves as Senior Director of Omnichannel Marketing. She has a deep passion for supporting her community through various channels, including PepsiCo's Hispanic ERG, ADELANTE; as well as the DFW Hispanic 100, a network of Latina leaders, and the Melville Family Foundation, which provides Black and Brown children in Dallas with financial, food, and educational assistance. Her husband and two children often join her to volunteer as a family.

LIZA OLIVA-PEREZ

"She believed she could so she did!"

She believed she could so she did! Looking back now, that is an understatement. Many years ago, I would have looked at things differently. Throughout life I've gone through so many trials and tragedies that looking forward to seeming dim considering my upbringing. About thirteen years ago, life took a turn that I never saw coming. In 2010, I lost my sixteen-year-old daughter to suicide, and it turned my world upside down. It took everything in me to keep going from day to day. However, I still had one young son that I had to tend to daily. He was my waking force and has kept me on track to where I am now. We went through some trials and tribulations but one thing we did was we never gave up. After losing my daughter I did not want to be the parent that I was. I wanted to be supportive, open, and accepting of my son so that he could live life as we never did.

Growing up in a very traumatic upbringing, I was surrounded by all forms of abuse. I did not want to continue those generational cycles, so I knew it was time to change. But it wasn't something I would learn from my mother. It got so bad that I truly hated my job and did not know where I was going next. Then after ten years of working in a not-for-profit named after my daughter, I decided that I wanted to work with students and make an impact. I was getting older, and I knew that to do something that I really wanted to do I may have to return to school. I looked at all my options and decided to return to school to become a teacher. Here I was, in my late forties, changing my whole life all around for the better.

After graduating with my Master's Degree in Education, I became a teacher in Chicago. Also, during this time, I had joined a leadership program for women; I then set goals for myself which was something I had not done in years. I set six goals, both personal and professional. I took this time to really look at life and work on myself. By the end of this program, I had accomplished five of my six goals. It took a lot of hard work and grit to get to where I am now. Some may think that some of these goals were minimal; but for me, they were giant milestones considering everything that we have been through. After losing my daughter I had lost my home, job, and partner of twelve years. Here I am, getting ready to hit fifty and doing all the things that I've wanted to do. If someone would have told me this would have been my life thirteen years ago when I lost my daughter, I would have thought they were crazy. But here I am, because I believed and I did it!

BIOGRAPHY

Liza Oliva-Perez is a multifaceted individual, embodying the roles of Mental Health Advocate, Real Estate Investor, Entrepreneur, Author, Educator, and Storyteller. As the Co-founder and Director of Operations at Simply Destinee Youth Center in Aurora, she leverages her personal journey after the devastating loss of her youngest daughter. Recognizing the pressing need for a supportive environment for young people, Liza is dedicated to mentoring, building confidence, offering peer support, and teaching positive coping mechanisms. Her firsthand experience of a traumatic upbringing has shaped her understanding of how trauma and upbringing influence our emotions, struggles, and resilience. With a Master's Degree in Education from National Louis University, Liza also serves as a compassionate teacher within Chicago Public Schools (CPS). She has an immense love of her husband, daughter, son, and two adored grandchildren.

FINDING MY PURPOSE IN A PLACE I CAN NOW CALL HOME

GISELLE ORTEGA

"Instead of wondering what if or what could have happened, take a chance on it; maybe that is where your destiny is."

Since my early childhood, I have had a strong passion for business and education. I believe we all deserve a prosperous future, and that future is in our hands. On the journey of building our future, finding someone to believe in us is important; but it is even more important to believe in ourselves.

After college, I came to the United States to learn the language, meet new people, and experience different cultures. I had my life well planned back in my country. However, God had different plans; and those plans were more fun and exciting than mine but full of challenges, sacrifices, and love.

I met my husband during my adventure in the United States, and the fight to make decisions began. Back in my country, I worked in a business incubator, helping entrepreneurs to develop their ideas into a business and to help small business owners to grow their businesses. After some time in my hometown, my father gave me a great piece of advice: "Instead of wondering what if or what could have happened, take a chance on it." So, I decided to return to the United States and take that chance. I have been married for fourteen years, and we have two beautiful boys, who are our motivation and inspiration to build a better future as a couple and family.

My husband and I have gone through all the challenges that any immigrant goes through in this country, but we decided that education was the foundation of our better future. I came to this country with a suitcase full of dreams; however, I arrived in 2009 without savings and without finding a job in my area of expertise. After some time, I decided to apply to graduate school, and I started a Certificate in Management program. At the end of my program, I received an invitation to study for a Master's Degree, and then "instead of wondering what if or what could have happened, I took the chance." I graduated with a Master in Business Administration (MBA).

After graduate school, during what seemed like it would be an easy transition, it was a challenge and a daily effort to find a job. After some time, I had to decide to continue looking for a job or to build my own opportunity. As an expert in business and following my passion for building a better future, I decided to create my own opportunity.

Nowadays, I have my own business, which I designed based on everything I am passionate about; it is another of my babies, which I have seen grow and develop. I love that it allows me to innovate, to evolve, to meet people, and to contribute to my community by creating jobs and through the services and experiences we bring to our customers.

Through my education and journey to find my dream job, I discovered my big passion; I want all people who come to this country full of dreams to fight for those dreams. The secret is to take advantage of your own skills and qualities. Education is key, and there are many resources that can help, but remember, we must remember who we are, be the best, and not give up!

BIOGRAPHY

Giselle Ortega was born in Mexico. She holds a Master of Business Administration (MBA) from the D'Amore-McKim School of Business at Northeastern University as well as a Bachelor of Science in Business with majors in Economics and Finance from the Sonora Institute of Technology in Mexico. Giselle has worked with many small businesses and nonprofit organizations to develop marketing strategies and find new, innovative market opportunities. An active member of the community, she has served as a marketing chair, adviser, and mentor for the Boston chapter of the Association of Latino Professionals for America (ALPFA) and the New England Association for Colombian Children (NEACOL). She also participates as a mentor for Women Who Empower from Northeastern University.

LINDA ORTIZ

"Being Latina, my experience has been like a recipe. It combines various ingredients and flavors to create a unique and distinctive taste. Both trials and tribulations have marked my journey, but also by strength, resilience, and pride."

Being Latina, my experience has been like a recipe. It combines various ingredients and flavors to create a unique and distinctive taste. Both trials and tribulations have marked my journey, but also by strength, resilience, and pride.

Like every great recipe has a base, so did my journey. My heritage and culture formed the foundation and roots of my experiences. My family, extended relatives, and close-knit community shaped who I am today. They instilled the importance of family, hard work, and tradition. From an early age, I was taught the value of respect for my elders, the power of storytelling, and the importance of music and dance in our culture.

As I grew older, I began to add my unique ingredients and flavors to the recipe. I discovered my passion for performance, public speaking, and social justice. My journey took me to college, where I learned about systemic issues affecting communities of color and ways to address them. I explored different corners of my identity and sought to amplify the voices of those who were disenfranchised.

While my journey had its share of successes, it was not without its challenges. Being a Latina in a predominantly all-male organization was tough. I often felt alone, isolated, and misunderstood. These also included facing discrimination in education, scarcity of opportunities, and battling imposter syndrome. But I never let my struggles deter me from continuing my journey. Instead, I used them as fuel to keep moving forward. I sought comfort in my culture, my family, and my community. I relied on the strength of my ancestors and the support of those who came before me.

When I felt lost, I turned to my recipe. I reminded myself that, just like when cooking, I had all the ingredients to create something beautiful. All I needed to do was follow the recipe. I recognized that the ability to blend the flavors of my traditions with the new experiences I gained was my superpower. I embraced my uniqueness in a world that often tries to homogenize everything.

I continued to perfect my recipe by seasoning it with determination and empowerment. I sought mentors and learned from their expertise as they shared their experiences as Latinas in their respective fields. I worked tirelessly to inform and educate others about the challenges facing communities of color, and I used my voice to advocate for meaningful change.

As I look back at my recipe, I am proud of the unique flavor it has taken on through the years. I am proud to say that my story includes my journey as a Latina. My roots taught me where I came from, while my journey taught me where I can go. When life throws me obstacles, I can navigate them with grace and resilience because I've had lots of practice. The recipe reminds me of my strength, worth, and magic.

So, I continue to add to my recipe, constantly experimenting with new ingredients and exploring previously uncharted territory while relying on my roots to guide me. Being a Latina will always be an essential ingredient in my recipe, one that I will proudly carry with me throughout my journey.

BIOGRAPHY

Linda Ortiz, a transformative leader in luxury brands with a passion for positive change, excels in fundraising and empowering women. Currently, she leads the strategic sponsorship/partnership for Women of Color in Fundraising and Philanthropy (WOC) while making waves in supporting a multi-million-dollar national campaign for The Paulist Fathers. Linda ignites progress as a Women in Development (WID) board member and Co-chair of WID's Communication Committee, and Chair of the Hispanic Alliance for Career Enhancement (HACE) New York Auxiliary Board. A licensed WomanSpeak Circle Leader Facilitator, she empowers women in public speaking and creates impactful voices. Linda holds a Bachelor of Arts Degree from Hunter College.

ELISE PADILLA

"I love the work I do at Rebel Leadership Group, LLC, because I get to rebel against systems of oppression, created by capitalist and patriarchal views of success that don't vibe with our traditional ways of living and giving."

With a compassionate heart and a desire to invest in the greater good, we enter into our careers as nonprofit or entrepreneurial leaders ready to make the change and be the change we know the world needs. Starry-eyed, we commit ourselves to a mission, a social service, to work that's important to us. But what happens when those starry-eyes dim? When the mission that drove us to our work has become distant from what we actually do?

I have worked in the behavioral health field for over twenty years, and over and again I come across leaders who started their journeys with passion and drive, but soon fell victim to burnout, compassion fatigue and profit-driven ideas of success. Unfortunately,

I was one of those leaders. I was overwhelmed, addicted, burnt out, depressed, all with anxiety that would put a trembling chihuahua to shame. When my mother pointed out the pain I refused to see, I knew something had to change. If not for me, then for my two young daughters who were building their lives based on the model I was providing. It broke my heart to realize that I was teaching them to prioritize money over health, work over passionate creation, and to put themselves and their needs last.

I had to re-learn as much as I could about myself and my roots, which meant rebuilding my life, my mental health and my career in a way that would ensure my daughters saw me embracing my authentic self and working to end a cycle of depletion. I founded Rebel Leadership Group, LLC, to support the supporters, heal the healers and provide embodied leadership to prevent burnout and compassion fatigue to those on the same path that I had been.

Now, I get re-energized by providing embodied leadership coaching and organizational support to non-profit leaders and entrepreneurs around the world, helping them develop strategy, intuition, and an authentic definition of success. I love the work I do at Rebel Leadership Group, LLC, because I get to rebel against systems of oppression, created by capitalist and patriarchal views of success that don't vibe with our traditional ways of living and giving.

Our mission, as rebel leaders, is to shift the collective mindset, leaving behind systems that once tore us down, creating new ways of living authentically, and embodying leadership principles that create healthy workplaces and businesses. The vision of Rebel Leadership, is that all people will know how to heal and find their authentic selves, guided by leaders who have blazed a new path of success built on community, compassion, abundance and faith. With this vision in mind, I know my daughters will be proud of the chains that I have broken and the return to the path of una alma serena.

BIOGRAPHY

Elise Padilla, MSW, MBA, CPSW, believes in the power of peer support and embodied leadership and uses her lived experience to support others in finding their authentic life path through her company, Rebel Leadership Group, LLC. Elise has been honored as a leader in mental health and has developed numerous successful nonprofit organizations. She's been overwhelmed, addicted, burnt out, depressed, all with anxiety that would put a trembling chihuahua to shame. She believes that we all have something to give, and by developing strategy and confidence, we can find success. Elise lives with her family in enchanting New Mexico.

ORIOL PAMIES CERVELLO

"It's amazing how you can transform what you hate about yourself into what makes you shine the most."

I was nineteen years old when I moved to Barcelona for college and I was excited to start a new life away from my hometown. I was born in Reus, a small city one hour from Barcelona, where practically everyone knows each other. With so many expectations about myself and what I was supposed to become in life, I was clear that being queer was definitely not one of them.

After years of sadness and self-hate I chose to take control of my life and start living authentically, being true to myself and who I really was. I decided to come out of the closet, although just with my close family and small group of friends, and move out from my family home and quit college.

I also decided to start my first business. I did not want any financial help from family and friends. I was ready to prove to everyone and myself that being gay didn't make me less. It was me against the world but something inside of me gave me the fire to fight. To hustle. And it was going so well! But starting so young into the entrepreneurship world made me an easy prey for those ready to take advantage of my innocence and inexperience.

One day, at age twenty-one, my business partner ran away with all our money, leaving me broke and responsible for company debt I suddenly had to answer for. "You should've stayed in college" was a sentence that rumbled in my head, but I was not ready to give up so easily. After nights of tears and endless months of hard work, I managed to repay everything and build myself back up.

I then decided to leave everything behind and move to Tel Aviv to explore new opportunities. Starting up your life from scratch alone, in a new country, with a different culture and language, so far away from home is tough. But those are the moments that define who you are. I started building a new business. But this time I wasn't running away from being gay but actually embracing it. And when you're on the right track, the universe just finds the way to lay things out for you. Magic always happens when you step outside your comfort zone and it was at that moment when I understood my true calling. Creating projects that allowed me to better the lives of people like me. To create job opportunities for those who are never getting a call back. To educate and shift mindsets creating a world that is more open, loving and diverse. I began building projects at the intersection between business and activism and it has been a catalyst for change in my life. It certainly has not been an easy way, but it has been my way.

There is no path to success other than trusting your intuition, being true to yourself, putting in the work and never listening to the nay-sayers. They are only projecting their fears onto you. Today, as you're reading this, I invite you to choose one thing that you're afraid of but you've always wanted to try. It's amazing how we are able to transform something we hate about ourselves into what makes us shine the most. And I'm excited to see your life turn around the moment you decide to take a life of faith and starting living your life on your own terms.

BIOGRAPHY

Oriol Pamies Cervello is a Spanish serial entrepreneur, LGBTQ+ activist, social media influencer, and internationally published author. He is Co-founder of the LGBTQ+ social app, Moovz, and joined the board of directors of the International Gay and Lesbian Travel Association (IGLTA). He founded Queer Destinations in 2019, a company focused on the promotion of LGBTQ+ tourism, developing an international tourism certification, which has expanded to Mexico, Spain, Holland, Panama, United States and Costa Rica. Later that year, Oriol also published his first book *Now That You Know*, an LGBTQ+ guide for the coming out process and on how to navigate the world being part of the community.

FOUNDATIONS OF GROWTH

BETTINA PASSOS

*"I now know that finding myself is really just returning to myself—
that I can balance the nostalgia with the need to go further."*

I never anticipated feeling nervous about the new environment
I found myself in when I moved to the United States. What I found
in the suburbs of Florida was so different from the mountains and
ocean in Brazil: endless streets littered with chain food places and
the local schools with their football stadiums that I believed only
to have existed in High School Musical. It doesn't sound exciting,
but back then it was the stuff of dreams. It was where I would find
the opportunities needed to grow, to go farther than the life I was
bound to in Brazil.

Maybe it's because I was young or because I was blinded by the
newness of it all. Maybe that's why I didn't blink when they said my
name was a bad word (Bettina, pronounced Be-tchi-na) or laughed
because I said "think" like "fink." All I knew was that to survive, I
was to move past what kept me tethered to Brazil, to forget all that
anchored me from moving forward successfully into American life.

I practiced the r's in my speech and read book after book, forgetting what it felt like to sound out words in my native tongue. I grew annoyed when my mother pronounced my name in Portuguese to the new neighbors, who insisted on emphasizing the "tch" in Bettina. Like my new name, I grew sharper, more precise, and calculated. It all paid off. I succeeded and made it past the Florida suburbs, into the city, and to a college I could have only dreamed of attending when I was younger.

Despite all the success, however, I grew unhappy. No matter how much I longed to forget the beauty of Portuguese, the feeling of waking to the birds singing their morning hymns to the mountains, I could not forget. We returned every year to visit, and each time I felt more disconnected from my reality. I was a gringa now, tongue-tied and shy, a girl who only thought and dreamt in English.

I felt as if my life was a tug of war between places—too American to be Brazilian, but too Brazilian to be American. Under the expectation to assimilate into a new culture, I had built up inaccurate conclusions of who I was meant to be. Now, however, after meeting and learning from those of different cultures, who fascinate me with their endless stories, I realized I have so much more to offer by allowing my culture to be a part of me. I am bound to return to Brazil, and I now know that finding myself is really just returning to myself—that I can balance the nostalgia with the need to go further.

I am now at a place where I have allowed myself to grow. I wrote a book on immigration, holding the stories I hear dear to my heart. I study International Relations in college, hoping to learn all I can to immerse myself into the vast interconnectedness of our world. Now, with Brazil and America in my heart, I grow.

BIOGRAPHY

Bettina Passos was born in Santa Catarina, Brazil, and moved to the United States when she was twelve years old. Growing up traveling due to her father's job, she was inspired to lead her academics toward the development and understanding of the world. After writing a book on immigrant stories, Bettina is pursuing a degree in International Relations at Claremont McKenna College. In the future, she wishes to focus her career on advocating for Hispanic and Latino success, hoping to use her roots as a pillar for her work.

AGOSTINA PECHI

"Let's embrace our heritage and ignite our passion. As Hispanic leaders, our voice, our vision, and our resilience have the power to change the future."

In the world of finance, I have had the privilege of standing out as a trailblazer, combining exceptional skills, visionary thinking, and unwavering determination. As a woman of Hispanic heritage, I have shattered barriers and made significant strides in a traditionally male-dominated industry.

EARLY LIFE AND HERITAGE:

I was born into a vibrant Hispanic family in Argentina, rich in culture and traditions. My upbringing instilled in me a deep appreciation for my heritage and a strong work ethic. Growing up, I lost my father and witnessed the struggles of my family, which motivated me to pursue my dreams fearlessly and to find a way to help them. This sense of heritage and resilience became defining characteristics in my journey towards a successful career in finance.

EDUCATIONAL FOUNDATION:

My commitment to excellence led me to pursue higher education in finance. I obtained a Bachelor's Degree in Economics from a prestigious university in Buenos Aires. My educational background laid the groundwork for my future achievements and solidified my understanding of global markets and economic trends. Upon graduation, I secured a position in a renowned investment banking firm. Despite it being a highly competitive and male-dominated field, my unwavering determination and strong leadership qualities helped me overcome any obstacles I encountered. My keen intellect, combined with my ability to navigate complex financial landscapes, quickly propelled me to prominent roles within the firm.

LEADERSHIP IN INVESTMENT BANKING AND CONTRIBUTION TO LATIN AMERICA:

As a female leader in Global Banking and Markets at Goldman Sachs, I have broken through the glass ceiling and helped to inspire countless women to pursue careers in finance. I have fostered a supportive and inclusive work environment, empowering my colleagues to excel. My innovative thinking and strategic decision-making have enabled me to guide high-profile investment deals, including financing programs for small and midsize enterprises

(SMEs) during the COVID-19 pandemic and structuring the first social bond (debt instruments) to provide access to social housing. Recognizing the untapped potential in our region, I championed initiatives that fostered economic development and created opportunities for local communities. My vision and commitment to sustainability have made a positive impact on various sectors, including renewable energy, infrastructure, and microfinance.

INSPIRING THE NEXT GENERATION:

We need to recognize the importance of inspiring the next generation of female leaders in finance. I actively engage in mentorship programs and speak at conferences, sharing my experiences and insights. By showcasing my Hispanic heritage and highlighting the importance of diversity, I encourage young women from diverse backgrounds to pursue their aspirations fearlessly, fostering a more inclusive and equitable finance industry. Let's embrace our heritage and ignite our passion. As Hispanic leader, our voice, our vision, and our resilience have the power to change the future.

As a female leader in investment banking and a champion of emerging markets, I have shattered stereotypes and paved the way for future generations. You can do the same.

BIOGRAPHY

Agostina Pechi is Managing Director at Goldman Sachs, responsible for Latin American and Caribbean Sales. She is focused on delivering innovation to the firm's clients across the global currencies and emerging markets, credit, rates and commodities businesses. Agostina is Co-head the Women's Network and is a member of the Steering Committee for the Firmwide Hispanic/ Latinx Network. She joined Goldman Sachs in 2013. Before that, Agostina worked at Credit Suisse and Deutsche Bank. Agostina serves on the Board of ProjectArt. She earned a Bachelor's Degree in Economics from Torcuato Di Tella University, has a daughter, and loves dancing the tango.

UNEARTHING EMPOWERMENT: A
JOURNEY THROUGH CULTURAL
IDENTITY

JOANNA PEÑA

"Our roots and culture are points of empowerment, not contention."

During my childhood in a vibrant Latino community, I had a strong sense of connection to my culture. Yet, a move to a predominantly Caucasian city stirred feelings of displacement. My high school years became a period of self-questioning and awakening, leading me to grapple with the disconnect between my Latin roots and my environment.

Such introspection sparked an empowering shift. I began to delve into my family history, drawing strength from stories of resilience and bravery. My multiculturalism transformed from a point of confusion into a badge of honor, a proud emblem of my unique identity. Despite skepticism and voices claiming I wasn't "Latina enough," I chose to rise, proudly affirming my Latinidad.

Harnessing my Puerto Rican and Cuban heritage, I

understood the significance of connection and community. This realization set the cornerstone for my career, guiding me to my role as the Multicultural Marketing Manager of the Eastern Region at Beam Suntory. Here, I weave the threads of diversity and inclusivity into a compelling narrative, echoing our multicultural audience.

I am devoted to fostering cultural harmony and embracing diversity in all aspects of my work. My drive to create positive change and connect communities is unwavering, and I recognize the critical role of bridging cultural differences in achieving this goal. I am committed to promoting inclusivity and unity, and I believe that we can make a meaningful impact by working together.

In our shared mission to inspire positive change, our diverse backgrounds should unite rather than divide us. Collaboration can nurture innovation, encouraging an equitable and compassionate world. This collaborative journey has gifted me with a valuable lesson.

Our roots and cultures should not be a source of contention but a wellspring of empowerment. As I stand today, I wholeheartedly embrace my Latinidad, advocating for Latinas and striving to bridge cultural divides. Our collective strength, passion, and diverse cultures deserve recognition and representation. Together, we carve out our rightful place at the table.

BIOGRAPHY

Joanna Peña, the Eastern Region's Multicultural Marketing Manager at Beam Suntory, is a proud Latina, a natural connector, and a steadfast advocate for cultural diversity and inclusivity. She has channeled this passion into ShakingFor, a 501c3 non-profit she co-founded to drive positive change and raise funds for multicultural communities in need. Joanna's journey, one of embracing her Latinidad, showcases her commitment to bridging cultural divides and shining a light on the beauty of multiculturalism. Her story is a powerful testament to self-acceptance, resilience, and the transformative power of connection.

ALEX PEREZ

"I'm lucky enough to have the privilege to help create a world where my children don't need to pick between two different ones but have the chance to build their own that lets them be 100 percent who they are."

My story starts somewhere I've never been—in the farmlands of Cuba. This is where my grandmother fought to get an education, even though her father didn't believe women belonged in schools. This is where my grandfather worked the sugar cane fields and was told he would not survive the fields. My grandmother never gave up and learned how to read and write even though she never stepped inside a classroom—becoming a political activist and author in the United States. She taught me the value of education and a growth mindset. My grandfather would not only survive the sugar cane fields but start a successful business in the United States and provide for his family and generations to come. He taught me the value of hard work and community.

My grandparents had been my version of the American Dream and my parents reinforced these lessons. I've spent my life trying to live by the values they passed down. I spent my youth focused on my education and working hard—believing I could out work any problem or obstacle. The hard work paid off and I was able to get into a great school and excel.

After school, I focused on the value of community and joined Teach for America to pass along the mindsets and opportunities given to me to others who needed that same chance. Two kids and a master of business administration (MBA) later, I found myself at Procter and Gamble, awestruck by the impact I could make and the opportunity to continue learning. Overnight, I went from impacting one classroom to impacting an entire country. I lead businesses that help create jobs in communities, deliver products that over half the country uses daily, and tell stories that help break stereotypes and help shape American culture. I couldn't be luckier or more grateful. On paper, I am the American Dream. But it hasn't always been a dream.

At each moment, it has felt like I've been living in two worlds—my Cuban background and the American one I needed to excel in. Each choice felt like I had to choose between my own culture or the chance to fit in and succeed. Those choices made me feel like I was too white to belong with my culture, but too brown to ever be fully accepted by the one I had worked so hard to succeed in. For years, I've thought of my grandparents. Would they be proud of what I accomplished or saddened by what I had to give up? What about my children—who are German, Irish, and

Cuban—and will they feel this tension even more than I have? And while I haven't quite cracked it, I do think that they would be proud. I'm lucky enough to have the privilege to help create a world where my children don't need to pick between two different ones but have the chance to build their own that lets them be 100 percent who they are. That is my American Dream.

BIOGRAPHY

Alex Perez grew up in New Jersey in a Cuban American household, where he learned the value of hard work, a growth mindset, and service from a young age. He received his Bachelor of Science Degree at Cornell University, spent six years in Teach for America, and then received his MBA from the University of Cincinnati. He is currently the Senior Brand Director for North America Laundry at Procter and Gamble, where he leads some of the biggest and most iconic brands—like Tide, Gain, Dreft, and Ariel—and tell stories that break stereotypes and make people feel seen and authentically represented. He lives in Cincinnati with his wife, Becca, and his two children, Emma and Max.

NEW BEGINNINGS

ANTONNY PORLLES

"New beginnings are like blank canvases waiting to be painted with the colors of your dreams and the brushes of your actions."

Migration has been a significant part of my life, starting even before my birth. My parents left Peru and immigrated to Japan, driven by the hope for a better future and greater opportunities. Their journey was far from easy, filled with challenges and moments of doubt when they contemplated returning. However, their unwavering determination to succeed outweighed those moments of weakness. Japan became my home for seven years, allowing me to immerse myself in its culture, appreciate its charm, and develop a profound understanding and admiration for the diversity surrounding me.

Upon relocating to Peru, a new chapter began, brimming with adventures and invaluable lessons, including learning Spanish. I immediately began experiencing life with an abundance of rhythm, color, and flavor. I swiftly fell in love with the country and its abundant offerings—the enchanting streets, breathtaking landscapes, vibrant folklore, warm-hearted people, poetic skies, and, of course, the unbelievably delicious food.

Peru unveiled the richness of its culture and exposed me to different realities I had never witnessed before. I encountered underrepresented individuals, who fought daily to provide for their families and sacrificed what little they had. Inspired to make a difference, I engaged in politics from a young age, assuming the role of National Representative of Youth Rights. My mission was to create inclusive spaces where the youth of Peru could be heard, as their voices were often silenced.

Collaborating with government organizations and UNICEF, we succeeded in being heard at the highest levels of power. We participated in radio and television interviews, and even made an impact in the president's house and congress. Our efforts bore fruit, as our work and civic responsibility were no longer underestimated, and the youth ceased being seen as merely the future but as active contributors to the present.

This experience revealed the untapped potential within each of us, emphasizing that consistency and perseverance are the keys to achieving the change we aspire to witness. Together, we can construct a more inclusive society that values diversity.

By a twist of fate, I had to relocate to the United States eight years ago. Frankly, when I received the news, I was at a loss for how to react, as it felt like I was relinquishing a part of my identity.

New beginnings greeted me—new streets, new landscapes— and with a smile, I embarked on a fresh journey, starting from scratch. I painstakingly learned English from the ground up until I could engage in coherent conversations. It wasn't easy; but gradually, I rediscovered the essence within me that propelled me to effect profound change for a country like never before.

I completed high school, pursued engineering in college, and graduated magna cum laude. Throughout my university years, I interned at prestigious Fortune 500 companies and served as the External Vice President of the Society of Hispanic Professional Engineers (SHPE), a prominent organization dedicated to empowering the Latino community in STEM fields. Our mission involved building bridges to access professional opportunities and fostering personal growth. I was honored with the engineering school's highest award, recognizing exceptional academic performance, community service, and leadership. Currently, I am employed at IBM, one of the world's largest technology companies, and this story is far from over. With certainty, I believe that I will continue to write more pages, accumulating experiences, and achieving further milestones, ensuring that my parents' unwavering efforts were not in vain.

Throughout this journey, I remain committed to embracing diversity and inclusion. The goal is not solely to secure a seat at the table but also to experience a sense of belonging. Together, we can accomplish even more.

BIOGRAPHY

Tonny Porlles was born in Japan but raised in Peru. He considers himself a positive and passionate individual, always embracing diversity and inclusion. After graduating from the University of Central Florida with a degree in Industrial Engineering at the age of twenty-three, Tonny joined IBM as an AIOps Automation Technical Solution Specialist in the Financial Service Market. He thrives on combining his sales and marketing skills with technical expertise to generate impact. Tonny has a love for exploring different food cultures, embodying a zest for life and a taste for adventure. As he often says, "Life is a buffet—savor every bite!"

NEO INDIGENOUS: A JOURNEY THROUGH STREETS AND SELF DISCOVERY

VICTOR "MARKA 27" QUIÑONEZ

"Art is more than self-expression; it drives change."

Growing up, I was drawn to graffiti, hip-hop, pop culture, and activism. I was also profoundly inspired by renowned Mexican artists and attempted to develop my style by blending contemporary and traditional elements with modern and indigenous aesthetics. For me, **art is much more than just self-expression.** It's a way to start a conversation, **drive change**, and give a voice to marginalized communities.

Through my art, I aim to highlight cultural identity, engage with people, and advocate for a better world. I always use my platform to empower underprivileged communities, and I firmly believe that art can make a difference. One of the things I appreciate about street art is how it brings people together. Whether a mural project or an installation, street art fosters community and belonging.

As an artist, I need to honor tradition, evolve, innovate creatively, and encourage awareness about social issues that matter. Art can initiate conversations, challenge people's beliefs, and inspire action. Whether it's addressing racism, sexism, or environmental concerns, it's important to use creativity for a positive difference in the world.

Design can be a powerful and impactful creative expression if a real purpose backs it. Street art is a way to make a statement and create an impact. It's a way to rebel, challenge the status quo, and give a voice to the voiceless.

Over time, I've developed my style, which I call "neo-indigenous." It merges my connection to Mexican art culture and heritage with modern elements of graffiti, contemporary design, and pop culture. My art is visually stunning as well as meaningful and thought-provoking. Art can catalyze change, and I always imbue my work with a sense of intention and purpose.

Reflecting on my life, I realize that street art has significantly shaped who I am today. It has allowed me to express myself, connect with others, and make a difference. I'm grateful for the opportunity to use my art to bring about change, and I'm excited to see what the future holds.

BIOGRAPHY

Victor "Marka27" Quiñonez is an internationally acclaimed street artist whose works blend contemporary art, graffiti, vinyl toys, fashion, design, and art activism. With Mexican heritage, Marka27 draws inspiration from legendary artists Diego Rivera, José Clemente Orozco, and David Siqueiros. His signature "neo-indigenous" style combines street and pop culture with Mexican and Indigenous aesthetics. Marka27's art promotes dialogue, cultural authenticity, and positive societal change, reflecting his belief in the transformative power of design with purpose.

BEING BETTER THAN YOU BELIEVE

STEVEN A. RODRÍGUEZ

"Life is 'not a marathon to be conquered but an adventure to be embraced with curiosity and resilience.'"

Contrary to the popular adage, life is actually nothing like a marathon. Sure, you have to be in it for the long haul, but that's only one piece of what life really is. It's actually more like a trial run, full of unexpected twists and turns, hills and valleys, and constantly changing landscapes. It's not a marathon to be conquered but an adventure to be embraced with curiosity and resilience. My own journey is a testament to this.

I still remember the day my parents learned about my college expulsion. It was a tough conversation, and I could see the disappointment in their eyes. But the pain of hearing my mother cry secretly in the basement sparked a change in me. I knew I couldn't keep running away from my problems and had to face reality.

It wasn't easy to go back to school after being expelled. I had to face the reality of my mistakes and work harder than ever to make up for lost time. I had to commute two hours each way and balance working part-time with studying and attending classes. But the pain of seeing my mother cry in secret pushed me to be better than I thought I could be. I learned to be resilient and focused, take things one day at a time, and appreciate every little victory.

Slowly but surely, I made progress. I earned good grades, acquired scholarships to cover tuition and study abroad programs, made new friends, and discovered interests and talents I never knew I had. I still had doubts and fears, but I learned to embrace them and use them as motivation to keep going. I realized that life is not about being perfect but about being better than you believe you can be.

After years of hard work, I earned my Associate's Degree and eventually completed my Bachelor's Degree. Although it wasn't easy, the effort paid off. Subsequently, I co-created entrepreneurial ecosystems across more than 170 countries, winning awards as a community professional and consultant. I also launched my own business, revolutionizing operations through a global LatAm talent network, and was acknowledged for my leadership commitment to the Hispanic movement.

Looking back, the pain and disappointment of my expulsion became a hidden blessing, compelling me to confront reality, tap into my potential, and grow into the person I am today. I've also written a forthcoming book titled, *Exponential Individuals,* aimed at assisting the next generation to achieve one's full self-expression.

Now, I want to share my story with others who may be facing similar challenges. I want them to know that life is not a marathon to be conquered but an adventure to be embraced with curiosity and resilience. And no matter how hard things may seem, it's never too late to turn things around and be better than you believe you can be.

BIOGRAPHY

Steven A. Rodríguez is a rising author and an award-winning community builder. He is a core member of the team behind Exponential Individuals. He is also a world-renown entrepreneurship ecosystem builder (across 170 countries) with diverse company RevOps experiences, including the Global Entrepreneurship Network, Techstars, and 1863 Ventures. His work blends across non-profits and universities, and he is a Partner at CrowdWork, a growing collective of fractional operators tackling global impact grants and challenges. Along with his wife, rising author Flor Liévano, Steven is Co-founder of OrangeUP Inc., a business venture revolutionizing operations through a global LatAm talent network.

A JOURNEY OF DREAMS: FROM VENEZUELA TO THE AMERICAN DREAM

ROBERTO RUIZ

"Sometimes we must take a route that may feel like it's going backwards to propel ourselves into the future."

Almost thirty years ago to the day I am sitting in front of my computer to write these lines, I looked out the window of the plane leaving Venezuela and swore to myself to never return. Next to me was my beautiful wife, Mercedes. Our dream was to move to a land of opportunity, to grow personally and professionally, and to start a family. We were excited and fearless. I came to do my Master of Business Administration (MBA) at George Washington University, leaving behind a successful early career, first in engineering and then in marketing. Our motivation was to leave a country in decline morally and economically, to one that we saw as a land of opportunity.

We worked odd jobs to support ourselves and studied full time. Mercedes learned English and quickly found a job. We were resourceful; I recall she had her mom send her wedding dress, which we sold for top dollar to buy a used car. I decided to rebuild my career in the United States and took a job as a Marketing Intern, after having had brand management positions at multinationals in Venezuela. The internship became a full-time job, I finished the MBA, and my career took off.

Looking back, I realize the power of accepting that sometimes we must take a route that may feel like it's going backwards to propel ourselves into the future. After the MBA, we moved from Washington, DC, to New Jersey to look for a better opportunity and access to the New York City job market. I became a partner at a top Hispanic ad agency.

We bought a home and started our family in New Jersey, where we moved to access their great public school system. Our strategy paid off and today we have two young adults pursuing their careers after graduating from top schools, Harvard and University of Miami.

Our journey is a true testament to the power of the American Dream. Two kids from Latin America who arrived with limited means, but with an education and a relentless desire to succeed. Thirty years later, I have a successful career in market research, and I am currently one of the highest-ranking Hispanics at the top Spanish language media company in the United States. Along the way we encountered many mentors, family members, educators, and friends who gave us opportunities and guidance.

We have learned a few lessons along the way. The first one is to always ask for what you want. Humbly and with education, one must ask so our desires materialize. The other is to build and care for relationships. It is the relationships we build that form the connections that will create possibilities, for us and for those around us. We should always build and nurture personal and professional networks.

Now the focus is on giving back, in mentoring and helping other immigrants realize the American Dream. During my career I have mentored several Latinos, who now occupy key roles in the media industry. I am forever grateful to this great country and its motto, "E pluribus unum." Out of many countries, cultures, races, one idea unites all of us—the American Dream is possible.

BIOGRAPHY

Roberto Ruiz is an accomplished research and analytics executive with a proven leadership track record. With over twenty years of experience, he has worked with global media companies, major consumer brands, and strategic consultancies, consistently delivering strong results. Ruiz earn his MBA in International Business and a Master of Arts in International Economics from The George Washington University, as well as a Bachelor's Degree in Mechanical Engineering from the Universidad Central de Venezuela. He actively speaks at trade conferences such as Association of National Advertisers (ANA), Consumer Technology Association (CES), Plan to Take on the World (PTTOW!), The Market Research Event (TMRE), The BeetTV Retreat, Cannes Lions, and Nielsen's Media 360, advocating for inclusivity and representativeness of Hispanics and minorities in research and data.

ALFREDO SANDOVAL

"Start NOW! And keep going!"

During the pandemic, while many people struggled with isolation and uncertainty, I embarked on a transformative journey that changed my life forever. My name is Alfredo Sandoval, a single father and former JP Morgan wealth manager. Graduating from Hofstra University in banking and finance, playing football in high school and college, I thought I had it all together. However, a wake-up call from my aunt during a visit to the Bronx, where she mentioned my weight, ignited a spark within me. Determined to be there for my two children, Caila and Blake, I knew it was time to break free from cultural norms and excuses. I had to rewrite my story, starting with my health.

For the first three months, frustration consumed me as I saw no visible results. I needed guidance, so I sought advice from individuals in great shape. To my surprise, the common thread among them was intermittent fasting. Inspired, I decided to incorporate it into my lifestyle and committed to two-a-day workouts. With gyms closed, I turned to outdoor workouts, embracing calisthenics and jumping rope as my go-to exercises. Day after day, I pushed myself, fueled by the determination to become the best version of myself.

As I persevered, the pounds began to melt away, and I witnessed the physical transformation taking place. During my workouts, I found solace in music that pumped me up and motivated me to keep pushing harder. Songs from the Rocky movies, hip-hop, Eminem's Lose Yourself, merengue, salsa, and Bad Bunny became the soundtrack to my journey. With each passing day, I became stronger, both physically and mentally.

Gradually, the scale started showing the results. Over the course of a year, in the midst of the pandemic, I shed an incredible seventy-four pounds. The impact of my weight loss extended beyond my own reflection in the mirror. It brought about profound changes in every aspect of my life.

One of the most heartwarming moments came when I noticed my twelve-year-old daughter, Caila, proudly holding my hand while walking in public. It was a testament to the positive influence my transformation had on my children. Furthermore, my professional life underwent a remarkable shift. The commitment to my health became a testament to my dedication and ability to care for others, opening new doors and opportunities in my career.

My story serves as a beacon of hope and motivation for anyone struggling with obesity or looking to make a positive change in their life. Breaking away from cultural norms that perpetuate excuses, I took charge of my health and rewrote my narrative. As a member of the Hispanic Latino community, I understand the influence of cultural traditions on our perception of food and self-care. By becoming more conscious of what we consume, we can redefine our relationship with health.

Through my journey of incredible resilience, perseverance, and determination, I have learned a vital lesson: the power of starting now. Not tomorrow or next week, but this very moment. Life is too precious to postpone our well-being. Let my story inspire others to embark on their own transformative journeys, for themselves, their families, and their communities. Together, we can change the narrative and build a healthier, happier future.

BIOGRAPHY

Alfredo Sandoval, a seasoned entrepreneur and accomplished business executive, is launching the highly anticipated *NYC Most Wanted* podcast in English and Spanish. With expertise in finance, technology, and sports, Alfredo brings unparalleled knowledge to this exciting venture. As the Founder and Co-founder of CaiFira, LLC, he has a reputation for identifying strategic business and investment opportunities for professional athletes and family offices in real estate and technology. With a background as a private wealth manager at JP Morgan Securities, Alfredo has provided comprehensive financial services to high-net-worth families, business owners, and athletes. Leveraging his experience, Alfredo is set to deliver engaging content through the *NYC Most Wanted* podcast, leaving a lasting impact on the business and sports communities.

ERICA PRISCILLA SANDOVAL

"Open our hearts to healing and immerse our souls."

What is a cacao ceremony? I shamed myself for not knowing this. I bet you don't either. Though I grew up in an Ecuadorian household and was born in Ecuador, I'd never heard of it. So I thought.

My abuelita made cacao, and it was delicious! She had an altar and prayed every day, but she never told me her secrets or plant medicine remedies. I would just drink what she gave me for my bronchitis and hold my breath. I forgot so many things about my childhood, perhaps because I was attempting to assimilate to the new world I was introduced to.

As I moved though my own journey, I realized that my success story is not based on all the degrees earned. It was not because I was the first in my family to graduate from college. It was not because I became an entrepreneur and author. My awards did not validate me. Instead, they humbled me because I knew I felt like an imposter when I assimilated. My success is rooted in my healing journey and how I owned my Latinidad and my purpose.

As a mental health professional with her own traumas, I knew our community needed more to heal than what's offered in traditional mental health spaces. I explored psychedelic trainings and was trained by the leading trauma experts. It was an expensive training with hardly any people of color in the room, yet we were talking about practices that came from indigenous communities. I knew I was in the right place.

I am proud to share that as I connected more with my roots, I became more successful. My love for my community became stronger, and I began to think of all the ways people can support themselves in their own healing journey. I knew we had to support destigmatizing mental health and incorporate ancestral practices.

I wanted to find a way to connect to healing my community in a way that looked different from sitting across from clients in an office and treating a diagnosis. In building community healing retreats, I've found my way back to my roots in a way that also nourishes my larger Latinx/e community and their holistic wellness. Together, we partake in cacao ceremonies, sacred medicines, sound healing, and ritual movement, ancestral practices that open our hearts to healing and immerse our souls in ourselves and our journey.

Integrating these ancestral healing practices into my work has made approaching mental health care more accessible for my community. They're healing in a space that values their entire personhood – especially their Latinidad—a rarity in Western mental health spaces. By expanding beyond Western healing norms, I've been able to reach people who've long been skeptical of mental health spaces. Now, they've embraced healing.

My childhood, society, and the social work profession all taught me that assimilation would make me successful and fulfilled. But really, all I had to do was return to my roots.

BIOGRAPHY

Erica Priscilla Sandoval, a licensed clinical social worker (LCSW), is an award-winning mental health practitioner, speaker, spiritual healer, podcaster, advocate, and four-time published author of Latinx/e in social work. She is the Founder and Chief Executive Officer (CEO) of Sandoval Psychotherapy Consultation—known as Sandoval CoLab—which offers talk therapy, community healing circles, ketamine-assisted therapy, and trainings in diversity, equity, inclusion, and wellness. Erica holds a Post Master's Degree in Clinical Adolescent Psychology and a Master's Degree in Social Work from the New York University Silver School of Social Work.

FROM STRUGGLING IMMIGRANT TO CHASING IRONMAN DREAMS

DORA SANTAMARIA-YAO

"Querer es poder," loosely translated as "Where there is a will, there is a way."

Growing up in Guatemala, life was basic. My father was a classical musician, and my mom a homemaker who also did odd jobs in sales and marketing to make ends meet. My parents told me to go to business high school to become a successful person's secretary. Dreams were nearsighted. I learned English in high school as being bilingual would give me more opportunities. They were right about that part! There were family problems and when I got a chance to come to New York as a high school graduation gift, I saw it as my chance for a better life and I took it.

I spent over a year doing odd jobs to survive, saving money to pay my mom back for the plane ticket and to help her with other debt. I saw the reality of hard-working Latinos, who were employed in stores and other low-wage jobs and were struggling like me. Deep in my heart, I decided that I had to work harder and smarter to advance my dreams. I wanted to make my parents proud. I believed that where there is a will, there is a way. So, I managed to save enough to enroll in a community college with a foreign student visa. I was able to work mostly to pay for tuition and barely made my living expenses. I then transferred to a four-year college, where I graduated with a Bachelor's Degree in Biology hoping to move on to a professional track. Then love happened.

I met a graduate student from China. It was love at first sight (at least my sight). We got married even when our future legal status was unknown. Through amnesty given to all Chinese graduate students in 1994, we both got our Green Cards. Life suddenly got safer and more promising. We had two children. Unfortunately, I became a single parent when they were young. Life or love is not always what it appears to be, so the next struggling journey began.

Parenting is hard. Single parenting is even harder. When my children were little, my heart was so broken, I was lost. I worked so hard at the office and at home at night. Days and nights blended into the other. Years passed. My life was passing by. In 2006, I decided that I had to do something to reinvent my career, so I went for the Project Management Professional Certification. I passed. Then in 2009, I decided I wanted to build a stronger future for myself, and I went for a Master in Business Administration (MBA) and graduated with honors in 2011. That set me off to a new professional journey at Northwell Health.

Professionally, I found my tribe at Northwell. Personally, I challenged myself to go beyond what I thought was possible, and I became a triathlete. I have been pursuing my Ironman dreams for five years, racing several events and completing two Ironman 70.3 races. I am up for my third one this year and full Ironman race next year.

Do not let others' expectations or opinions limit you. Believe that you can, and you will.

BIOGRAPHY

Born and raised in Guatemala, Dora SantaMaria-Yao (also known by her middle name, Nineth) immigrated to the United States at age seventeen to pursue the American Dream, which she could not clearly define at the time except that it had to do with better opportunities. Despite many hardships, including discrimination, she always had a don't-give-up attitude. With personal resolve and determination, she completed her college education, got a Master in Business Administration (MBA), has a professional career, and raised a family mostly as a single parent. But she's not done yet. Her dreams keep growing and evolving every year overcoming barriers with a "Si se puede" attitude.

THE ART OF LIBERATION: EMBRACING ANCESTRAL WISDOM FOR SOCIAL CHANGE

YURA SAPI

"Reconnecting with ancestral cultures and traditions, we heal from the trauma of colonization and build a better future."

As a first-generation Ecuadorian and Colombian American growing up in the suburbs of New York, I was immersed in the allure of the American Dream. My parents worked tirelessly to provide for our family, instilling in me the expectation to follow in their footsteps. However, as I grew older, I began questioning the systems at play. I couldn't ignore the inequities and injustices that existed all around me. I knew I had to do something to make a change.

In the pursuit of dismantling oppressive structures, I founded Advancing Arts Forward, a movement dedicated to advancing equity, inclusion, and justice through the arts. With a graduate degree in Performing Arts Management and a thesis focused on diversity, equity, and inclusion (DEI) initiatives, I had spent a year working full time in the "dream" as a Diversity and Inclusion Coordinator at Actors Equity Association. But the reality of Broadway didn't match the glamour portrayed. The organizational hierarchies and the glacial pace of change disappointed me. I felt like I was selling out my ability to truly "do something" impactful. #TheRevolutionWillNotBeFunded

Feeling trapped and dependent on one organization for my livelihood, I made a bold decision. I left everything behind and traveled to Ecuador and Colombia, immersing myself in the cultures of Indigenous and Black communities, seeking to understand anti-racism beyond a US perspective. Something was calling me to engage with my ability to bridge worlds.

In 2021, I found myself in Nuquí, Chocó, a remote region of the Colombian Pacific coast accessible only by air or sea. There, I connected with the Earth, rediscovering ancestral practices and immersing myself in sustainable living. Octavia Butler's *The Parable of the Sower* became my guiding light on this transformative journey.

Advancing Arts Forward, now expanded to a full-blown 501(c)(3) nonprofit called LiberArte, Inc., holds space for marginalized people to ignite initiatives for creative activism, create impactful art, and reconnect with their ancestral cultures on the global scale. Through international artist residencies, podcasts, and multidisciplinary experiences, we strive to heal from the legacies of colonization, capitalism, and white supremacy.

As a proud Indigenous Kichwa descendant, I aim to pave the way for decolonized leadership and foster borderless global solidarity through the arts. By reconnecting with our ancestral cultures and traditions, we can heal from the trauma of colonization and build a better future. I aspire to inspire others to join me in the fight for justice and equity, creating a world where anyone can make an impact and use their privileges for the betterment of our world.

BIOGRAPHY

Yura Sapi is a visionary leader, creative activist, and interdisciplinary artist, who promotes anti-racism and decolonization for a globally just future. As the Co-founder and Chief Executive Officer (CEO) of US nonprofit, LiberArte Inc., Yura builds racial, social, and climate justice worldwide through empowering artists and creative activists. One of Yura's most significant contributions is the Building Our Own Tables podcast, which they host and produce. They offer racial, gender, and disability DEI consulting as part of the Melanin Collective and host workshops, discussions, and coaching programs worldwide. Yura's work reflects their deep commitment to promoting collective liberation and advancing the cause of healing as true justice.

THE MURALS OF MY JOURNEY: COLORING THE WORLD WITH CULTURAL BRIDGES

EDWIN "DON RIMX" SEPULVEDA

"Making something in public is a bold move. It means you have the drive to create and are willing to share it with the world."

As a young boy, I found myself immersed in the vibrant culture of San Juan, Puerto Rico. The city's colorful surroundings, lively music, and pulsating energy inspired me to express my love for my culture through art. Using the walls around me as my canvas, I painted the vivid life of Puerto Rico, drawing from the radiant hues of the Caribbean, the rich history of my people, and the unique intricacies of our culture.

Through my art, I discovered the transformative power of public art. My first mural project showed me that my creations were more than murals—they were cultural bridges. They connected people, places, history, and the future, sparking conversations and fostering connections. Seeing the spark of curiosity in passersby and the sense of shared ownership, they developed was truly eye-opening. This reaffirmed my passion for art and its ability to inspire change and connection.

Looking back on my journey, I see a collage of rich experiences, each mural forming a unique piece. The immense joy and fulfillment of doing what I love is priceless. I've learned that art is a powerful catalyst for conversation, change, and connection. It's not just about creating aesthetically pleasing visuals—it's about weaving stories that captivate the intellect and stir the soul.

Each mural is a declaration of my love for my culture, my roots, and my community. It's a medium to share the beauty of my Latinidad with the world, inspire, evoke thought, and kindle a dialogue. Creating in public spaces is a testament to my commitment to expose myself wholly, to vulnerably share my process, ideas, and essence through my art. That fills me with hope for the future.

I am incredibly fortunate to have had the opportunity to make significant contributions to a wide range of public art projects. Each project presented its own unique set of challenges and opportunities, and I am proud to say that I met each one head-on with enthusiasm and creativity. Being a part of these projects has been an absolute joy, and I am thrilled to have positively impacted the communities they serve.

As I continue to create and share my art with the world, I am reminded of the power of storytelling and cultural expression. Through my murals, I inspire others to explore their roots and appreciate the beauty of diversity. I am grateful for the opportunity to share my passion with others and to be a part of a movement that celebrates unity and connection. My art is a reflection of who I am, where I come from, and where I hope to go. And it will continue to inspire, uplift, and connect people for years to come.

BIOGRAPHY

Don Rimx, also known as Edwin Sepulveda, is a renowned Puerto Rican artist. He creates murals that blend art and culture, reflecting his lifelong passion for the arts. Don has received formal training in fine arts and has become a master in his craft. His murals pay homage to the history and culture of the places he paints, sparking meaningful conversations within communities. Don believes in the transformative power of public art and produces captivating pieces that embody his vision and unite diverse audiences.

MY VOICE MATTERS AND MY STUDENTS MATTER: ADVOCATING FOR MULTILINGUAL LEARNERS

ALYSSA SILVA-RAFI

"I was asked what my students' families need. I realized I AM the expert in this room. I am the EDUCATOR. I felt empowered and I felt a responsibility to my students."

I packed my bags and jumped in the minivan with my daughters, Aaila and Alanah in the backseat, my husband driving, and our adorable lizard, a bearded dragon named Leo. We were off to Washington DC.

A few months earlier I received an email about attending the Teachers of English to Speakers of Other Languages (TESOL) International Association Policy Summit. At the end of the summit, educators would have the opportunity to go to Capitol Hill to advocate for multilingual learners. I cannot explain my overwhelming feeling when I saw this opportunity. It was as if someone was telling me I was meant to go.

I am an advocate for my students and families in the classroom. I know I am making an impact in the classroom. Part of me knew I wanted to take that passion and advocate for my students and ALL multilingual learners. The imposter syndrome kicked in. Why me? I am just a fourth-grade Latina teacher from Chicago. I am not a principal; I am not a superintendent. Who am I to go to DC and speak to legislatures about education?

We arrived and drove straight to the Lincoln Memorial. I watched as my girls rode scooters down the National Mall. Being there with my family just felt right.

The summit experience was life-changing. It was inspiring to be with other advocates for multilingual learners. I was paired up with Dr. Gina Johnson Wells from Illinois. I cannot thank her enough for taking me under her wing during the summit. Then came the day when I went to Capitol Hill. I will never forget the feeling. I partly felt like a fangirl as I looked for people I recognized from CNN or people I have read about in articles. It felt inspiring just to be in the buildings and watch the hustle and bustle of important business going on around me. Again, the imposter syndrome set in. Why am I here? I am just a fourth-grade teacher from Chicago.

It was time for the first meeting. When we sat down, I was asked where I was coming from. I was so nervous that I decided to just be natural and be myself. I told the legislative assistant that I drove in my minivan with my family and my pet lizard to come to advocate for my students. He instantly softened. He asked me about the drive and Leo the lizard, and I relaxed. I shared statistics and trends about why we need to fund and support multilingual learners, but then I just started talking about my students. I shared stories about what I do in the classroom and why the federal government has a responsibility to support the students I teach every day.

After each meeting, I felt more comfortable, my voice became more comfortable, and it felt like a natural call to action. I was asked what I needed for my students; I was asked what my students' families need. I realized *I AM the expert in this room.* I am the EDUCATOR. I felt empowered and I felt a responsibility to my students. That day helped me realize that my voice matters, and I can use it outside of my school community because my students matter.

BIOGRAPHY

Alyssa Silva-Rafi is an elementary school teacher for Chicago Public Schools with a commitment to working and advocating for multilingual learners. She received her Master's Degree in Curriculum and Instruction with an English as a Second Language (ESL) endorsement. She is currently working towards a Leadership PhD with a specialization in Curriculum and Instruction. She also mentors first-year teachers across the district and is a Virtual Instructional Coach for the We Care Mentoring Program. Alyssa serves as the Elementary Special Interest Group (SIG) Chair for Illinois Teachers of English to Speakers of Other Languages-Bilingual Education (Illinois TESOL-BE). Alyssa was a 2023 Those Who Excel and Teacher of the Year awardee receiving an award of Special Recognition in the teacher category from the Illinois State Board of Education.

SUSAN TENORIO

"I am grateful for all these experiences, both good and bad, as they have bestowed wisdom upon me and shaped me into the person I am today."

I could feel my face growing warm and my eyes welling up as I said my goodbyes at the farewell brunch my family organized for me in South Florida. It was difficult to bid farewell to everything I had known—my family and friends. In that moment, I held tightly onto my faith and reminded myself of the reasons behind my decision to move away. I was confident that one day, I would achieve my goals of purchasing a home or homes, excelling in my career, and that this move into the unknown would be one of the best decisions of my life. I packed up my belongings and tossed them into the backseat of my car, unaware that it would be a life-changing moment and the last time I would see my family together in one place. I hungered for growth, opportunities, connection, and success. I have always been highly ambitious and possess a strong desire to excel in life. I strive for success in all my endeavors, and I wish the same for those around me.

After the move, I found myself in a completely new world, facing numerous challenges along the way. I suddenly realized how much I missed my family gatherings, the Latin culture, and the tropical climate. For the first time, I felt alone and isolated. As time passed, I discovered that I had entered into one-sided friendships and toxic relationships. It took some time for me to realize the impact they had on my self-esteem and confidence. That's when I decided it was time to regain control of my future. I became acutely aware of the company I kept, picked myself up, wiped away my own tears, and surrounded myself with a strong community of people I respected and aspired to be like.

Through various organizations, I began connecting with women who excelled in their careers and personal lives. They became my mentors and, without knowing it, helped me overcome everything that tried to break me. I learned the importance of recognizing my worth, speaking up, clearly expressing my desires, and not settling for less than I deserve. I was determined to push through the uncomfortable moments and always find the light in every circumstance. Gradually, I regained my confidence and self-esteem. I am grateful for all these experiences, both good and bad, as they have bestowed wisdom upon me and shaped me into the person I am today. My motivation has always been rooted in the sacrifices my parents made when they came to the United States to provide my sister and me with a chance at a better life than they had. This brings me to one of my favorite quotes from Carmen Boullosa, "I can and I will. Watch me."

My journey has taught me that the circle of people you surround yourself with greatly influences your success. It is crucial, at any stage of life, to be surrounded by like-minded individuals, who share the same values and interests. By sharing my story, I hope to inspire others to pursue their dreams and persevere through challenging times.

BIOGRAPHY

Susan Tenorio, a Wealth Management Specialist at Merrill Lynch, is a community connector, leader, and first-generation college graduate from a Colombian background. Ten years ago, she bravely relocated from South Florida to Atlanta, Georgia, seeking personal and professional growth. Susan's passion for serving others is evident through her engagement with the Association of Latino Professionals for America (ALPFA), where she held leadership roles as Events Director. She has organized charity walks, toy drives, and mentored survivors of homelessness, human trafficking, domestic abuse, and exploitation. Co-founding a Latin Employee Resource Group and FlourisHER mentorship program, Susan leverages her expertise to drive meaningful change and create a better future for her community.

ALEJANDRA GARCÍA TORRES

*"Born with brown hair, brown skin, brown eyes, the first name
Alejandra and last name García are appropriate. At first glance,
I am just like the name I was given, simple and common. But
at second, and third, and fourth glances, it is discovered there is
more to me and my name."*

My parents gave me a simple yet strong name: Alejandra
García. I was born to Mexican parents, who crossed the border in
their youth, immigrants in a strange land. Born with brown hair,
brown skin, brown eyes, the first name Alejandra and last name
García are appropriate. At first glance, I am just like the name I was
given, simple and common. But at second, and third, and fourth
glances, it is discovered there is more to me and my name. How
often though, do people actually take a closer look?

Being Mexican American is just as uncomfortable as it sounds. A clear division of identity is always present. One of the common challenges is not knowing how to answer the question, "Where are you from?" Simple question, right? Not for me. Are people asking where I was born? Do they want to know my race? Where I currently live? Depending on the question, my answer will be different. This question though, is minor to bigger challenges.

I spent my childhood in California, a liberal state where we could feel safe. Mexicans, Blacks, Middle Easterners, and Whites all got along in school. Our classrooms were colorful and our diversity was rich. Then my family and I moved to a small Texas town, where it felt like segregation still existed. I even joke around saying I didn't know I was Mexican until I came to Texas, as it felt like I was always reminded by my peers. I didn't like this division and refused to only socialize with Mexicans. Seeing that I was friends with White people, the Mexican students, started saying I was White-washed— like bread: brown on the outside, white on the inside. Later in college, my professors wanted me to join their organizations, run for leadership, and apply to scholarships. I was ecstatic, until they would say things like "As a young Latina, you could win" or "We need more people like you in our club." Suddenly the integrity of my merit would be gone.

People often think I am more comfortable with Spanish than English. Not so. My first words were Spanish, but around age seven onward it has always been English. For many years, I stopped speaking Spanish completely and was accused by my family and others of having denied my heritage. But English is meaningful to my identity, especially in writing. If my culturally proud Mexican parents can admire that, then so should the world.

I think of my own children, young and hopeful, not yet aware of the boxes people will try to fit them in. Maybe they will find themselves in the similar situations. And yet, I haven't lost hope. I think back on my name; how common it is, but also how strong it sounds. My name is Alejandra García and my identity is full of contradictions. But then again, so is everyone's. We all just need to take a closer look.

BIOGRAPHY

Alejandra García Torres is a rising creative copywriter with a passion for weaving together the perfect words. She's led a career in communications and education. Alejandra has been a content editor, copywriter, copy manager, reading/writing teacher and professional communications teacher. Her natural storytelling ability, advanced writing-focused degrees, and knack for finding typos help her write the ideal words that draw attention. She's written for business to business (B2B) and business to consumer (B2C), startups, e-commerce, elected officials, nonprofits, professionals, and more. No matter the topic, Alejandra stays true to her motto: Write the way people speak and you'll be amazed at how you can grow your audience.

GEORGE TORRES

"Everything I do, I do with love . . . love and sofrito, that's all you need."

Six weeks after Hurricane Maria ravaged Puerto Rico in 2017, I found myself in a modest house on a mountainside. Alongside a few of my college buddies, I joined a mission to help provide humanitarian aid to the remote regions of the island, delivering meals, provisions, medical assistance, and mental health services to those in need.

The hardest part of this trip was listening to people who felt broken. We listened empathetically and tried, if nothing else, to let them know we were there for them. It was sad . . . but I was also grateful and felt privileged to be in a position to serve. In this experience, I found inspiration from my grandmother, Gloria, who taught me the importance of service and kindness.

My grandmother, affectionately known as Mama, was a social justice warrior who sought to serve God as a nun. However, a summer romance led to the birth of my mother, Carmen Gloria, altering her path. Despite this detour, she lived her life in service to others. Mama raised me during times when my mother couldn't, and we often engaged in conversations about our rich cultural history and the disparities in the communities we lived in.

During our kitchen conversations, Mama emphasized the significance of having a strong foundation, both as individuals and as a people. I vividly remember asking her what made her food taste so good, and she replied, "Everything I do, I do with love . . . love and sofrito, that's all you need." This analogy became a cornerstone of my life's work, as I founded SofritoForYourSoul.com.

Sofrito, the foundation of Puerto Rican cuisine, represented the essence of our culture. I carried her wisdom with me, knowing that love and a pinch of our cultural heritage could bring solace and nourishment to those in need. These words remind me of the profound impact one person can make, of the power of love to heal and uplift, and the strength that lies within our roots. Mama's wisdom taught me that without it, life would be lacking. I realized that I could carry on her legacy through community building and storytelling, using technology as a tool to connect and uplift others.

As I stood on a mountain, rain gently falling on my face, and the sun's rays illuminating my cheeks, the elderly woman I was delivering food to exclaimed "Se casa una Bruja!" an expression Puerto Ricans jokingly use to describe a weather phenomenon that could only be described as magic. It felt like a magical moment, as if Mama herself was speaking to me. It was then that I realized my actions were unknowingly carrying on her grassroots legacy, honoring her memory through my work. It was even more revealing that at that very moment, I was doing it her way: door to door, one person at a time with a delicious meal prepared with Sofrito.

In my journey, I carry the torch of my grandmother's legacy, spreading love, compassion, and memories of the sweet smell of sofrito wherever I go. Mama was right, we can make a difference, one act of love at a time.

BIOGRAPHY

George Torres is an award-winning storyteller and talent agent, whose mission is to connect Latinos to their cultural identity via new media. He founded SofritoForYourSoul.com, the first Latino cultural blog in 1997. Known as "Urban Jibaro," he is described as a pioneer and community builder who is unafraid to create new spaces to amplify the voices of the Latino diaspora. Whether it's established brands, emerging artists, small businesses or non-profits, George understands how to bring cultural relevance to the forefront. In 2022, he acquired a partnership stake in Talento Unlimited, a Miami based boutique social media agency.

LET FAILURE FUEL YOUR SUPER POWER!

DINAH TORRES-QUIÑONES

"I will not be defined by one failure because success isn't final, and failure isn't fatal."

When I share my story, I feel a flood of emotions, nothing out of the norm for a self-identified empath—we're always in our feelings. The more I want to share my successes and triumphs with you, the more I understand that for you to contextualize the level of my success, I have to first expose the truth about my, brace yourself—here comes the f*bomb—my Failures! Yes, with an S, as in plural.

To FAIL—It's that four-letter word that gets judged harshly and leads to another four-letter F*bomb, FEAR! My failures have lived at the intersections of my Success and Storytelling, but the greatest lesson I have learned through failing is that I can let it turn into fear and paralyze me, or I can use it as fuel and let it catapult me.

These days, when I walk into a room, I am introduced as Dr. Dinah Torres-Quiñones; it is truly a humbling moment. I am a Humboldt Park born and bred, West Side of Chicago Puertorriqueña. Today, I am one of five chiefs in my organization. I completed my graduate studies at a Big Ten University, Northwestern University, a Wildcat for life! In the middle of a global pandemic, I founded a consulting firm to help individuals and small nonprofits learn research administration and grant acquisition processes, as well as provide organizational and individual executive coaching.

While I am deeply proud of these accomplishments, I never forget that I am also the girl who was once a high school dropout. I privately grappling with my father's drug addiction and the adverse impact his substance abuse was having on my mother, my younger siblings, and me. I struggled significantly and ultimately failed to finish high school. I still remember sitting across from a school counselor as she told my mother, "Your daughter will never amount to anything more than driving a preacher to drink!"

The counselor's words and my failure lived on my skin, making me feel like an embarrassment to myself, my family, and my community. Yet, I am immeasurably grateful for a group of extraordinary women, including my mom, who, despite my many failures, did not allow that to be the end of my story. Instead, they extended me grace and showed me that if I leaned in to failing fast and failing forward, I would find my superpower, and I did— **Persistence!**

Their encouragement and guidance allowed me to understand that my failure was only one element of my story, but it wasn't the whole story. I will not be defined by any one of my failures because success isn't final, and failure isn't fatal. Now, I see failure as an opportunity to Find An Invaluable Lesson Using Real Experience and, through it, grow my inner strengths and values to meet the goals I aspire to in meeting others where they are and helping them to where they want to go!

BIOGRAPHY

Dinah Torres-Quiñones' truth is a journey of discovery that intersects at three fundamental pillars, faith, culture, and servant leadership. Her path has charged her with passionate work advocating for health and education equity and creating bridges, where there were once barriers. She is the Chief of Staff at Humboldt Park Health and the Founder of DTQ Consulting. She has experienced the power of strategy, collaboration, communication, and advocacy in changing her life from high school dropout to graduate scholar. With her Doctoral Degree in Healthcare Administration, she meets people where they are and helps them get to where they are going!

IDENTITY UNLEASHED:
PERSEVERANCE, COMMUNITY, AND
SELF-DISCOVERY

CATHERINE GRACE TREVIÑO

"There is a village that stands with me through every success story."

I was an invincible little girl who joined every and any school extra-curricular activity, was scrutinized in elementary for being "the social butterfly" of her class, and was determined to be a computer engineer. That was my identity for as long as I could remember.

I did not have many computer courses in my public-school journey, but I sure loved to try and learn new things. However, it felt like that little girl inside of me started to slip away while I was in the chair in the office of my university adviser, swelling with tears after hearing, "Engineering is just not for you." All the dreams and goals that I had been working for seemed to be so out of reach, right at that moment. Sobbing, thoughts began to swirl in my head like, "Maybe I can try being a *insert any other career here*" trying to find my so-called passions in little spots of interest I had in my mind. I was not afraid of rejection or failure, but I was afraid of being a quitter.

I had to reach out for help, so I started with my inner-circle friends and family. It's amazing how everyone said the same thing in different ways, "Try again." My parents and grandparents supported me going back home and trying the same major in a different school. My experience there was drastically different. I started to find pieces of myself again in leadership roles at my local university, helping others find their way by becoming a tutor for a digital systems course and then leading an organization to bring job opportunities to my peers. I saw a path for my career as I began my journey into corporate as an engineer, but I couldn't do it alone. Being a first-generation corporate employee means that there are situations and questions I have that can't always be answered by family and friends. I looked for mentors and sponsors to develop a community in my career space. There is a village that stands with me through every success story.

As I continue to grow through a multitude of similar experiences, I've realized that my identity is not tied to a specific career or characteristic, but rather having the perseverance to fight through doubt and be anything I set my mind to through support of community and lift up others in the process.

BIOGRAPHY

Catherine Grace Treviño is a passionate Technical Brand Specialist at IBM, providing technical consultation to clients in Financial Services Markets. She holds a Bachelor of Science in Computer Engineering from the University of Texas Rio Grande Valley. As a Society of Hispanic Professional Engineers (SHPE) lifetime member, she co-created a virtual conference for Latinas in science, technology, engineering and math (STEM), inspiring over 250 individuals. Catherine continues to promote diversity in STEM through her work and leadership in the Familia@IBM group, organizing events and co-creating the WAAH+IBM Latinos of Impact Webinar. She is recognized for her advocacy for diversity in STEM and mentorship, featured on SHPE, SHARE, and Business Insider.

WATER BEARS AND OUR INNER STRENGTH TO PREVAIL AGAINST THE ODDS

GLENDA VALERO DE SILANO

"I've learned we can't predict how much bitter and sweet we get in life, but we can control our mindset and attitude to make the journey a memorable one."

My daughters Cristina and Maria once told me, "Mami, your call-sign is the water bear!" I needed a call-sign for an office activity. Puzzled by their suggestion, I asked why, "It's a micro-animal able to survive extreme conditions." They explained "Mami, you're resilient and do it all: you take care of us, work hard, help others, you are a good friend, and never lose hope. That's you!" My heart melted.

I'm Venezuelan and the eldest of three siblings. Papi was an insurance agent and Mami a stay-at-home mom. Though neither graduated from college, both taught me the meaning of hard work. Dad was strict and continuously reminded us that that despite not having an inheritance to leave behind, he would do anything for our education. He pushed me hard on my grades and sacrificed a lot for me to attend a good university, learn English, pursue a double major; he believed I could do more.

I started my professional career as a Human Resources Administrative Assistant. A scholarship was the only way to continue my development and get a Master's Degree in Human Resources (HR) in the United States. That year, I got the only full-ride Fullbright scholarship in Venezuela. I couldn't believe it! I quit my job and took a chance as a newlywed with my husband, Ramon, and started a new adventure.

After graduation I rejoined my former employer and today, twenty-three years later (and counting), my career has taken me to unimaginable places. From a rookie admin assistant to an HR Director, eleven moves including living in four different countries, I've been fortunate to have great mentors, sponsors, and teams who have been my greatest supporters. As I've climbed up the ladder, so has the huge responsibility to continue delivering and using my voice and commitment to open the doors for others shooting for the stars.

But for me it's never been *just* about work. I've been blessed with a fulfilling personal life with a twist of sweet and bitter. Sweetness exemplified by the birth of my children and seeing the world through their eyes, visiting many places around the world, meeting special people who have become long-lasting friends and part of our global family. Bitterness was due to losing both my parents within two years of each other, being displaced from our flooded home during Hurricane Harvey, and shortly after dealing with the passing of my baby daughter Viviana. I've learned we can't predict how much bitter and sweet we get in life, but we can control our mindset and attitude to make the journey a memorable one. Though I've been on my knees emotionally several times, faith and a solid support group have refilled my resiliency tank.

I'm convinced everyone has survived extreme conditions, but perhaps not given themselves credit for it. Remember you're not supposed to go through life alone. I haven't! Though we all may be water bears inside, never forget to rely on others to bounce back, keep working and achieving the impossible.

You've got this!

BIOGRAPHY

Glenda Valero de Silano is a proud Venezuelan, married, and mother of three. She is a runner, a heart health champion, and HR Director at Chevron with more than twenty-three years of experience. She joined Chevron in 1997 and has held HR positions of diverse scope and complexity with resident assignments in Kazakhstan; Canada; Houston Texas; San Ramon, California; and Venezuela. She also has had twenty-three years of engagement with the Somos Hispanic and Latino Employee Network and is currently serving as an Executive Sponsor. She has been a Board Member of the Chevron Federal Credit Union since 2022. Glenda earned a Bachelor of Science Degree in Political Science, a Master in Science in HR Management, and is a Fullbright alumna.

ALEXANDRA VENNERI

"I realized in walking the dilapidated streets of Havana that not everyone can control their circumstances but can only strive to make the best of their situation."

In 2018, I had an opportunity to travel to Cuba with my husband for the first time. It was the fiftieth anniversary of my mother's immigration from Cuba and the fifty-fifth anniversary for my father. As a first-generation Hispanic American, born in Miami, I have always had curiosity of my familial roots and wanted to understand more about post-revolution Cuba and why my family left in the 1960s. One of the activities I was most excited about prior to my trip was taking a walking tour of Havana with a Cuban Economist, Jorge. We learned the average Cuban makes 30 Cuban convertible pesos (CUC) monthly, while doctors have the highest salaries around 80 CUC. For perspective, a liter of drinking water is 1 CUC, gallon of oil or beer is 2 CUC. Because of the extreme lack of means provided by government mandated salaries, Cubans have what I like to call a side hustle or as the Cuban people say a "buscador."

Jorge shared stories on private businesses, education, healthcare, and media. All incredibly fascinating topics that ended with a common denominator, suppression of freedoms. Whether suppression comes in the form of limiting news, entertainment, flexibility to explore different opportunities with your degree, or guaranteed access to care when needed, all things I know I have taken for granted in my upbringing in America. I have always prided myself on working my hardest and striving to live up to the success of my immigrant parents. I realized in walking the dilapidated streets of Havana that not everyone can control their circumstances but can only strive to make the best of their situation.

We ended our tour in the home of Jorge's abuela, Teresa. She shared stories on the marvelous pre-revolution Cuba and the post-revolution seizure of private income and property to the government that eliminated the financial security and freedoms her family previously experienced. In asking Teresa why she never left Cuba, her response is family. She has family that fled and has not been able to communicate with them since. Before we left Teresa's home, Jorge poured everyone on the tour a rum and Coke or what the world calls a "Cuba Libre." In English this translates to a "Free Cuba." Cubans have another name for this drink, they call it a "Mentirita," which translates to "little lies." Cuba Libre es una mentira, and I am incredibly grateful to my grandparents for having the strength and fortitude to leave Cuba when they did. Reminiscing on what unites myself as a first-generation American to Cuban people, I think on the importance of family; the ability to work hard for everything we have, even if you need to find a side hustle; and having a passion for life, regardless of your circumstances. I can easily say that every member of my family has experienced true freedom and is better off in the United States and traveling to Cuba was eye opening to that reality.

BIOGRAPHY

Alexandra Venneri is a first-generation Cuban American living in Cincinnati, Ohio, with her husband, Beau; son, Asher; and Bernese Mountain dog, Ellie. She is a Brand Director at Procter & Gamble, striving to provide better health outcomes for America's smiles with Crest toothpaste. She leads Procter & Gamble's Latina Women's offsite connecting over three hundred Latinas to networking and professional development opportunities. She has a passion for traveling (especially to Miami to visit family), cooking, collecting wine, and playing tennis.

LUIS VILLA-ALCAZAR

"Our story shows that everyone possesses the ability to achieve their dreams. For Hispanics however, it is not despite our background, but because of it, since we have the resilience and strength to pursue them."

Born in El Paso, Texas, and raised in Juarez, Mexico, I had never fully embraced the identity of being Hispanic. Instead, I saw myself as a "border boy," straddling the line between two cultures without fully understanding the power of the Hispanic community. I unintentionally isolated myself as a Mexican who happened to be born in the United States.

Destiny introduced me to Carolina, who, with compassion and determination, has dedicated her life to various humanitarian causes. Carolina's global experiences and unwavering commitment to serving the less fortunate resonated. Recognizing my resilience and potential, she became a mentor and a catalyst for change for me.

Carolina's vision extended beyond borders when she shared her plan to move to New York City, where she would continue her work with Mexico's Permanent Mission for the United Nations. She invited me to join her on this journey. Eager for new opportunities and motivated by her belief in me, I wholeheartedly accepted.

My transition to New York City was uncertain, but we faced it head on. As we navigated the bustling streets and embraced the vibrant multicultural fabric of the city, I felt a profound sense of awe and that we were in the right place. Our community became our family, offering guidance and support as we settled into our new lives, even by helping me to secure a job.

At work, the importance of affordable housing preservation became my passion. Drawing from my own experiences of the struggles faced by marginalized communities, I dedicate myself to advancing affordable housing initiatives.

Through resilience and unwavering determination, we've flourished and formalized our commitment to each other in marriage. We continue to pursue our personal and shared goals, motivated by the belief that together, we could achieve more than we could have ever imagined independently. My journey from a struggling orphan in the border region of El Paso and Juarez to a successful professional in the bustling metropolis of New York City stands as a testament to the power of hope, love, and the belief that one person can make a difference. Our story resonates with countless others who may feel marginalized or constrained by their circumstances.

As Hispanic individuals, we embody the spirit of the American

Dream leaving behind everything familiar to pursue a brighter future. We embrace the opportunities that arise while honoring our cultural heritage and striving to create a more inclusive society.

Our journey demonstrates the transformative power of finding the right community, which believes in your potential and is willing to help you along your journey. We learned that with a shared vision, we can make a lasting impact and create a better world for future generations.

Our story shows that everyone possesses the ability to achieve their dreams. For Hispanics however, it is not despite our background, but because of it, since we have the resilience and strength to pursue them. By embracing diversity, working collaboratively, and supporting one another, we can build a society where everyone has equal opportunities to thrive.

BIOGRAPHY

Born in El Paso, TX, and raised in Ciudad Juárez, Luis Villa-Alcazar went to Catholic schools in Mexico and then enrolled in the University of Texas at El Paso (UTEP) to pursue a Bachelor of Business Administration (BBA) in Economics. His professional journey is in real estate, pursuing a passion for urban development. Starting as a property manager in Texas. Later, driven by love, relocated to New York City to join his now-wife and ventured into Asset Management. In their journey from the border, they realized that being Hispanic is not simply cultural heritage but a diverse and vibrant community with a collective power.

FROM BEING LOST TO BEING AN ENTREPRENEUR

DELIA VISBAL

"My success is a testament to my hard work, resourcefulness, and unwavering belief in myself."

My story is one of resilience, determination, and personal growth. I made the courageous decision to pursue better work opportunities and safety in the United States (US), leaving my family behind. I embarked on a journey that would shape my future in unforeseen ways.

I studied economics and experienced a stressful and underpaid job in Colombia. Initially, I faced challenges in the US, encountering a toxic relationship that hindered my progress. I found myself working various jobs just to make ends meet. However, after experiencing depression and self-reflection, I found the strength to leave the relationship and moved to New York City to pursue my dreams.

My path in New York City was not easy. I took on various jobs, including working at Macy's, cold calling at State Farm, and taking on administrative roles. But I remained determined and eventually landed a job as a Legal Assistant at a small law firm. After a year, I sought better opportunities that aligned with my skills and aspirations.

Overcoming self-doubt due to English not being my native language and my limited experience, I secured a position as an Assistant to the legal team at a tech company. This opportunity exceeded my expectations, offering great benefits and a salary that seemed unimaginable before.

However, I lost my job when Microsoft acquired this company and had only two weeks to find a new job. Yet, through my involvement in the Latin Employee Resource Group, I received support and encouragement from my colleagues, which ultimately led to an Account Manager position in the sales team.

I was laid off again this year as part of the tech industry mass layoffs, but I quickly secured a new and better job in another tech company. Today, I reflect on my journey with gratitude and a sense of achievement. I never anticipated working for such prestigious companies. My success is a testament to my hard work, resourcefulness, and unwavering belief in myself.

In addition to my professional accomplishments, I co-founded Pure Joy Coffee, an online Colombian specialty coffee company, with my boyfriend. We not only offer roasted coffee beans but also Corporate Coffee Tastings and Mindfulness Workshops to promote diversity and create a positive workplace culture. My entrepreneurial spirit and dedication to creating a happy life extend beyond my career.

As I continue to pursue my dreams and set high goals, my biggest aspiration is to have my family join me in the US, allowing us to be together and cherish valuable moments. With my US citizenship already achieved and the process initiated for my parents' immigration, my journey is a testament to my determination to create a better life for myself and my loved ones.

Above all, my story highlights the power of resilience, hard work, and self-belief in overcoming obstacles and achieving happiness and success. My unwavering commitment to personal growth and pursuit of my dreams serves as an inspiration to others facing similar challenges.

BIOGRAPHY

Delia Visbal was born and raised in Barranquilla, Colombia. I am Generation Zero, meaning she was the first person of her family who immigrated to the US from Colombia eight years ago when she was twenty-seven years old. Today, her whole family still lives in Colombia. She studied economics in Colombia and worked in a stock brokerage company assisting traders. However, this job was very stressful, demanding and not well paid. This, plus the fact that she had recently broke up with her boyfriend, made her decide to leave her country to pursue a job opportunity for a better quality of life.

'MI HIJA HARD WORK PAYS OFF' FROM SMALL FARM TOWN UPBRINGING TO BUILDING WORKFORCES IN GEORGIA

MARIA WHITFIELD

"While herding cows may be more physically demanding, herding people can be mentally exhausting."

My name is Maria Whitfield, the Director of Workforce at the Savannah Harbor-Interstate 16 Corridor Joint Development Authority (Savannah JDA). I feel incredibly fortunate to be living the American Dream, as I hail from a small farm town with a population of less than 500 in southern Colorado. Never in my wildest dreams did I imagine that I would end up building workforces, traveling to foreign countries, and leading teams. But here I am, rocking it out in the human resources (HR) field for nearly three decades now.

My Hispanic heritage and upbringing have played a significant role in shaping my work ethic, career path, and personal journey.

My father with an eighth-grade education and mother with a tenth-grade education would have never dreamed what success their kids would have. I still remember moving cows from one pasture to another. While herding cows may be more physically demanding, herding people can be mentally exhausting. For the past twenty years, I've been building workforces and working in human resources in the surrounding counties of Savannah, Georgia. Through my tenure, I've gained extensive experience working with several local startup international manufacturing companies and even had the opportunity to work in Germany, which was an amazing experience.

I remember the early days of my career when I often found myself as the only Hispanic person in the room, not to mention, the only woman at the table. I felt pressure to prove myself and work harder than my peers to earn their respect. Despite these challenges, I refused to let imposter syndrome hold me back. My dad's words constantly echoed in my mind, "Mi hija, hard work pays off."

I've had an impressive career journey, working in various HR roles throughout my career. I started my career as a Human Resources Assistant nearly thirty years ago and have diligently worked my way up the corporate ladder in various positions to my current role as the Director of Workforce for an entire region. I have always had a flair for being creative and am known for thinking outside of the box. Building relationships with people is what drew me into HR in the first place.

In my most recent position, I was hired as the Director of Workforce for the Savannah JDA. The creation of this role was prompted by the area's substantial expansion, which was driven by Hyundai's plans to construct the world's largest electric vehicle plant, resulting in the addition of more than 10,000 jobs. My job is to work with existing industries in the region to identify their workforce needs, address labor supply challenges, and develop programs to address workforce challenges. Pressure? Yes, but will I die? No. But I will die trying.

I've never lost sight of my roots or my passion for building relationships with people. I have always been the biggest cheerleader for those around me in their career journey. I feel a sense of responsibility to help lift others along the way.

BIOGRAPHY

Maria Whitfield, the Director of Workforce at the Savannah Harbor-Interstate 16 Corridor Joint Development Authority, is a successful Hispanic professional who has built workforces for over twenty years in Savannah, Georgia, gaining extensive experience in her tenure. With a flair for creativity and a talent for building relationships, Maria has worked her way up the corporate ladder all over the world from HR Assistant to Director of Workforce. She oversees a regional workforce study that is helping to develop programs to address workforce challenges. When not working, Maria enjoys blogging, traveling, and supporting her children at their sports games.

ISAAC YANEZ

"Despite all my obstacles, failure will never overtake me if my determination to succeed is strong enough. I am willing and capable of continuing to rise to greater heights by demonstrating discipline in the right steps, and I will eventually shine as a Hispanic star."

I began community college later than most people, and I debated whether to major in psychology or neuroscience. I majored in neuroscience because I wanted to learn about and to conduct research on the biological basis of behavior. Despite having to take more classes for this degree than psychology, I was determined to finish it. COVID-19 occurred when I transferred to The University of Texas at Dallas (UTD), making it much more difficult to gain lab experience. This, along with my online experience and some of my professors, discouraged me from pursuing an advanced degree in the field. Because I only had a Bachelor's Degree in Neuroscience, I knew my options for neuroscience-related jobs were limited after graduation.

So, I considered what I could do and looked up the Edwin L. Cox School of Business at Southern Methodist University (SMU) in Dallas. I was interested in the Master in Science (MS) Degree in Business Management because I thought it would help me in the job market. However, because I found out about the MS program late, I enrolled right before the program began, so I had to catch up on program and coursework prework. Looking back, I might have missed out on SMU consulting industry prep sessions if I had enrolled before summer 2021. Nonetheless, I was adamant about finishing the MS program. Unfortunately, my father became ill and died at my house at the start of the program, so I had to deal with negative emotions as well as the finances of my family's estate. I considered dropping out because I had fallen behind on my coursework, but my schedule had been altered to accommodate my unfortunate situation.

In the second semester of my Master's Program, I began looking for work. My career coach primarily assigned me different roles, but they could have been a more effective mentor when it came to analyzing my education and experience to guide me toward the right role. This is one of the reasons I've struggled with my job search. Other reasons include a lack of corporate internships; not connecting as deeply with my cohort as I had hoped; inactivity in professional organizations, such as the Association of Latino Professionals for America (ALPFA); and a lack of a stronger network to leverage. Furthermore, I recently discovered that I could be considered neurodivergent, but if I manage it properly it makes me an asset for organizations and society. Despite all my obstacles, failure will never overtake me if my determination to succeed is strong enough. I am willing and capable of continuing to rise to greater heights by demonstrating discipline in the right steps, and I will eventually shine as a Hispanic star.

BIOGRAPHY

Isaac Yanez, who was raised in Dallas, Texas, is Mexican American and an only child. He is a first-generation college graduate. He is humble and eager to assist and mentor anyone. He enjoys learning new things and being as creative as possible.

EL VOLCÁN

CHRISTIAN ZANI

"Life is a journey, not a destination." – Ralph Waldo Emerson

At the age of twelve, I had the amazing opportunity to climb Volcan de Agua in Guatemala with my father. The 12,000-foot volcano towers above the city of Antigua, creating a wonderful backdrop and one of the most recognizable landmarks of the country.

Agua is every hiker's dream. Even with the right equipment, the treacherous incline can be challenging, but not impossible. The extraordinary views from the top are nothing like I have ever seen. Despite this amazing experience, the climb also brought many challenges. Challenges, which have taught me some life-long lessons, have served me well in my career as an Executive Recruiter. This was the first time my father and I had climbed any kind of mountain! We didn't have any proper hiking gear, boots, or backpacks to facilitate our journey.

The first valuable lesson I learned on this trip is that preparation is key! Without preparation, study, or an understanding of the journey in front of you, reaching the destination or end goal will be much more complicated than necessary. This doesn't mean you won't be faced with obstacles, but preparation will help you navigate those challenges along the way. After nine hours, we reached the coveted summit. Despite the scrapes, bruises, and intense exhaustion, I was able to sit, rest, and appreciate the view of majestic emerald valleys, peppered with surrounding volcanoes.

The second valuable lesson I learned was to stop and appreciate the result. Many times, we fail to treasure the "wins" in our lives and accomplishments. Regardless of how big or small the accomplishment is, there is value in taking time to recognize those achievements and the achievements of others. It's easy to dismiss accomplishments. As leaders, we should be mindful to recognize the achievements of our team and colleagues.

After spending the night on the volcano, it was time for our descent. The return was much quicker and perhaps more complicated than the climb. I vividly remember falling twelve times! Most of the tumbles I experienced were due to the lack of proper footwear. There were other instances where the narrow trails were difficult to navigate.

The third valuable lesson learned on this journey is the importance of picking yourself up. Fortunately, my father was there to motivate and encourage me. No matter where you are in your career or life journey, it's imperative to pick yourself up after your fall or fail. It's also important to recognize the need to help and encourage others through those difficult times and challenges.

Years later, during a very difficult hike in Colorado, a good friend reminded me that our hike and life was more about the journey and not the destination. Those words truly resonated with me then and today. Wherever you are in life, or your career, take the time to prepare. But don't forget to appreciate the accomplishments and challenges along the way; and no matter what, whether you slip, fall, or take a few steps back—pick yourself up and keep going!

BIOGRAPHY

Christian Zani is an Executive Search Lead and Diversity Advocate within IBM's Global Executive Search and Integration team. He is responsible for identifying and attracting Partner-level talent to the firm. Prior to IBM, he served as Project Manager for Korn Ferry and spent more than six years as an Executive Recruiter with EY. He is originally from Buenos Aires, Argentina. He also lived thirteen years in Guatemala, where his family served as missionaries. Christian currently resides in Dallas, Texas and is married to his beautiful wife Liliana, who is from Mexico, and a proud stepfather to Andres and Braulio. Christian is an avid musician, producer, and writer. He also loves the opportunity to volunteer, serve in his church, mentor, and coach others.

ABOUT THE AUTHOR

Claudia Romo Edelman is a social entrepreneur, an advocate and a catalyst for change. A captivating public speaker and media contributor, Claudia is a leader of inclusion, focused on unifying the U.S. Hispanic community and promoting sustainability and purpose-driven activities.

Claudia is the Founder of the We Are All Human Foundation, a New York-based non-profit foundation, dedicated to advancing the agenda of diversity, inclusion and equity. She is also a Founder and Co-Host of 'Global GoalsCast', a podcast which highlights global progress through the stories of champions making a difference.

With an extraordinary background with global organizations, including the United Nations and the World Economic Forum, she has worked on humanitarian causes for 25 years with organizations such as UNICEF, the UN Refugee Agency (UNHCR) and the Global Fund to fight AIDS, Tuberculosis and Malaria.

Prior to her role at the We Are All Human, she was seconded to the Executive Office of the Secretary-General of the United Nations to lead communications and advocacy for the Sustainable Development Goals (SDGs), which she was instrumental in their creation and launch.

ABOUT THE PUBLISHER

Jacqueline Ruiz is a visionary social entrepreneur that has created an enterprise of inspiration. With more of 20 years of experience in the marketing and Public relations industry, she has created two successful award-winning companies, established two nonprofit organizations, published 32 books, the largest collection of Latina stories in a book anthology series in the world, and held events in four continents. She has received over 30 awards for her contributions and business acumen. She represents the 1.6% of women entrepreneurs with over seven figures in the United States.

Being a two-time cancer survivor activated her sense of urgency to serve others and live life to the fullest. Jacqueline is one of the few Latina sports airplane pilots in the United States. Visit www.figfactormedia.com and www.jackiecamacho.com for more information.

Made in USA - North Chelmsford, MA
17718_9781959989738
10.13.2023 1027